Virtues of
INDEPENDENCE
and Dependence
on Virtues

I0095081

Virtues of **INDEPENDENCE** and Dependence on Virtues

Ludvig Beckman
Emil Uddhammar
Editors

Routledge
Taylor & Francis Group

LONDON AND NEW YORK

First published 2003 by Transaction Publishers

Published 2017 by Routledge
2 Park Square, Milton Park, Abingdon, Oxon, OX14 4RN
711 Third Avenue, New York, NY 10017, USA

First issued in paperback 2018

Routledge is an imprint of the Taylor & Francis Group, an informa business

Copyright © 2003 by Taylor & Francis.

All rights reserved. No part of this book may be reprinted or reproduced or utilised in any form or by any electronic, mechanical, or other means, now known or hereafter invented, including photocopying and recording, or in any information storage or retrieval system, without permission in writing from the publishers.

Notice:
Product or corporate names may be trademarks or registered trademarks, and are used only for identification and explanation without intent to infringe.

Library of Congress Catalog Number: 2002020275

Library of Congress Cataloging-in-Publication Data

Virtues of independence and dependence on virtues / Ludvig Beckman and Emil Uddhammar, editors.
    p. cm.
    Includes bibliographical references and index.
    Contents: Roots / Göran Lantz—Reverence, respect, and dependence / Paul Woodruff—Aesthetic experience and virtue / Katarina Elam—Autonomy's sources and the impact of globalization / John Dunn—Personal independence and social justice / Ludvig Beckman—Autonomy and moral responsibility / Göran Möller—The politics of virtue in the French Revolution / Ruth Scurr—Volunteering as virtue / Bryan S. Turner—The relation between independence and trust / Emil Uddhammar.
    ISBN 0-7658-0173-6 (alk. paper)
    1. Virtue. I. Beckman, Ludvig. II. Uddhammar, Emil, 1957-

BJ1521 .V585 2002
179'.9—dc21   2002020275

ISBN 13: 978-1-138-51777-6 (pbk)
ISBN 13: 978-0-7658-0173-9 (hbk)

Contents

Preface

This is a book about virtues, in particular the virtue of personal independence. The subject can be introduced by considering the few who are endowed with an abundance of this virtue, e.g. the heroes of fiction, movies, and popular culture. Typically, heroes are not only strong and powerful, but also virtuous and independent. To some extent, this combination of character traits is paradoxical. This is so because modern heroes—whether we are speaking about Superman, the X-Men, or Batman—have few social bonds but are at the same time exceptionally virtuous. Typically, fictional heroes have no citizenship, and few friendships or relationships; they don't, so to speak, belong anywhere. Still, they care for, fight, and protect a lot of people. Heroes are virtuous, strong, and independent, but seem to be in no need of relationships, emotions, or virtues to maintain these dispositions. This is the real sense in which the fictional hero is superhuman. Where people usually depend on others, and gain strength from their relationships, the fictional hero is able to create moral power from nowhere.

A clear illustration of this paradox is found in the late-1970s movie *Mad Max*. With a post-apocalyptic setting, it is a story of the last remaining site of civilization, Bartertown: a city fuelled by waste, built by slaves, an unhappy marriage of primitive technology and terror. In this chaotic and violent place we find the leading character of the movie, Mad Max, who is, unsurprisingly, an exceptional figure. Mad Max has the capacity to resist the norms of brutality that reigns in Bartertown and brings to this savage world something hitherto unknown: independence and virtue. The conflict with the rulers of Bartertown is inevitable, but the heroic dispositions of Mad Max eventually prove victorious. Mad Max destroys the evil forces and points out the direction of a new and better world which, alas, he is unable to share.

Despite the hostile nature of the world, Mad Max is able to maintain personal independence and virtue. The question naturally arises:

What are the sources of his virtues? People watching the movie cannot expect to find an answer to this question. At a more general level, however, we hope that the readers of this book will. The ambition of this work is to explore the nature and the sources of the virtues of personal independence.

The assumption we accept as a point of departure is that personal independence is a distinct good, a virtue, of the modern, Westernized age. Whatever people may strive to realize in their lives—fame, wealth, social status, or immortality—there is a widespread conviction that each person has the right and privilege to articulate his or her particular vision of the good life. In this sense independence, understood either as autonomy, authenticity, or individuality, remains a fundamental value of our culture.

Yet, independence is not the sole virtue recognized in our societies. It will consequently be of interest to clarify the relation between the virtues of independence and other aspects of society. Thus, our subject calls for both normative and empirical analysis.

By normative analysis we will be able to decipher the conflicts between different norms, reasons, and values that are involved in the attempt to harmonize distinct virtues. When and why is independence valuable? Is the urge for independence something to regret or applaud? And how can we adjudicate when independence conflicts with other virtues?

By empirical analysis we will be able to describe and explain the relationship and manifestations between the virtues of independence and other phenomena. An important empirical issue is to clarify the empirical conditions of personal independence. More in tune with Confucius' teachings, and less in the spirit of the movie *Mad Max*, we assume that virtues must have "neighbors." In fact, the idea of an organized society where people have no sense of goodness, tenderness, helpfulness, or bravery—where the notion of more or less worthy attitudes or behavior is absent—is not just horrifying but probably also incoherent. Thus, despite momentary acts of terrorism and violence, the world as we know it is inhabited by people whose virtues keep the world going round. Virtue is not at home in the wastelands of terror. This is also why Mad Max is such an exceptional figure. In sum, we need to ask questions about the viability of personal independence. To what extent does the achievement of independence depend on the existence of other values and social practices?

As should be clear, speaking about virtues is not the unique privilege of the moralist. The category of virtues is a possible starting point for the systematic study of human values and behavior. Because the virtues are essential ingredients of our societies, we should take seriously the task to explore their dynamics, complexity, and value.

Besides this claim, we are making two more assumptions. First, virtues are part of ordinary life. The virtues are not primarily philosophical or abstract notions, but very much part of regular social life. Secondly, the virtues are a helpful category in the search for knowledge of the social world. The virtues do not simply constitute useful objects of study. There is also a heuristic value in bringing the notion of virtue back into the methodological arsenal of social and human sciences. It enables us to pose a number of new and pressing questions about our society.

One of the key arguments of Alasdair MacIntyre's now classic *After Virtue* was that the success of analytical philosophy in the twentieth century undermined our faith in questions concerned with the meaning and contents of the good life and the virtues. The validity of MacIntyre's thesis has been questioned and argued ever since. The most fascinating fact is, however, that MacIntyre's work can now be seen as a part of a broader movement that effectively has transformed the agenda of social and philosophical thought. As a consequence, the often-repeated thesis, that the virtues have been neglected, is no longer as true as it may have been.

In this volume, a prominent collection of scholars in politics, theology, philosophy, sociology, and aesthetics examine the *contexts*, *challenges*, and *consequences* of the virtues of independence. In the first section we find the contributions of Göran Lantz, Paul Woodruff, and Katarina Elam. Though working in different disciplines and tackling distinct questions, they have a common theme: the idea that ethics depends on virtues and on the social or cultural practices that make them possible. In a very literal sense then, it is argued that the virtues provide the *context* for ethical reflection.

The contributions to the discussion of the second section are written by John Dunn, Ludvig Beckman, Göran Möller, and Ruth Scurr. The aim of these essays is to assess the value of personal independence. Are we sure that this fashionable virtue should always be promoted? And how do we handle the *conflicts* that may occur between independence and other virtues?

In the last section, Bryan S. Turner and Emil Uddhammar examine the virtues of the empirical world. What is the social and political significance of personal independence—and of virtues more generally? Through the lens of sociology and political science we are thus provided with a qualified view of the *consequences* of personal independence.

We would like to thank the City University of Stockholm and the Axel and Margaret Ax:son Johnson Foundation for the generous support which made this work possible.

Ludvig Beckman and Emil Uddhammar
Stockholm, Sweden
February 2002

1

Roots

Göran Lantz

"The Need for Roots" is the English title of an essay by the French philosopher Simone Weil.[1] It was written in France during the turbulent times of the Second World War. Weil is searching for roots in the history and faith of the French working class and of the French nation at large. "Roots" is, of course, meant in a metaphorical sense. And the use of metaphorical language in philosophy is both necessary and legitimate. Allow me to make use of the same metaphor, but partly for other purposes. I will use the metaphor "roots" in a sense related to that of Simone Weil when, at the beginning of her essay, she maintains that duties are primary to rights: being rooted is to have taken on duties and responsibilities, to be tied to other people by bonds of love, affection, common interests, and common projects of different kinds. These are bonds of duty and commitment. But my special concern is to demonstrate why man is necessarily rooted also in external objects and in places.

The Roots of Ethics

Ethics—moral philosophy—without roots, is abstract ethics; it is reductionist.[2] That is, it is not rooted in presuppositions about human nature and about man's place in the world. It considers moral problems as they occur, in abstraction from their human context. It focuses upon "thin" concepts such as right, wrong, duty, etc. Utilitarianism is the paradigm example of such abstract, reductionist ethics, but also Kantianism comes close to it.

What then is an ethics with roots? It is the exact opposite of reductionist ethics. This type of ethics is situated in a kind of anthropology

1

and in a broad historical and social context. It is situated in the "land-scape of ethics," to allude to the Swedish title of a work by Göran Möller.[3] It considers moral problems in their broader social setting and in their longer time-perspective. It is concerned with moral institutions (e.g. forgiveness, tolerance, promise, property) and with "thick" concepts such as family, nation, home, care, health, illness, and so on. Whereas utilitarianism and Kantianism and other kinds of principle ethics can be described as merely criteria of right and wrong or as decision-methods (or both), a "rooted ethics" takes an interest in the human conditions for acting morally. The former kinds of ethics suggest necessary and sufficient conditions for moral rightness, but the latter also has something to say about how to bring about moral conduct. In this respect virtue ethics comes nearer to the ideal of a "rooted ethics."

Consider the complicated web of human life, the vast fabric of manifold relations between individuals and associations of people. Further consider the pretensions to formulate in one sentence, in one criterion, an all-covering guide to moral human behavior. This undertaking must appear horrendously bizarre.

Compare this web of human life with an ideal piece of art. It depicts life as manifold, complicated, even full of contradictions—as real life is. Why then should an individual life project be simple and possible to capture in one ideal principle? And ways of life are what morality is about: excellence of one's personal life project.

Non-rooted ethics is searching for an Archimedian point from which to build morality. It aspires to build an ethical system from scratch. To my mind this is futile. We always have to start with an existing moral tradition and with existing moral institutions. Here the philosophical parable of the broken ship seems appropriate. The ship cannot be brought to a dock to be rebuilt. It must be repaired at sea by exchanging plank after plank. Take, for instance, medical ethics. Utilitarian ethics may start afresh by suggesting conditions for killing or rescuing patients (and it certainly does). In my argument, it ought rather to start out from the existing (and very strong and vital) traditional professional ethics of doctors and nurses and then in a critical way scrutinize and improve them. Let us call this strategy "critical traditionalism." Critical traditionalism is about mapping out the moral landscape, investigating the intricate web of relations and bonds between individuals and groups of individuals, and improving existing moral institutions.

If Hegel's concept of "Sittlichkeit" represents morality as lived and incorporated into social institutions, then critical traditionalism should focus upon precisely Sittlichkeit.

Anthropology and the Need for Roots

There is a link between a view of ethics as built upon abstract principles and a view of man as an atomistic, rational, and egoistic being. It is most obvious in utilitarian ethics. Both its strength and its weakness are precisely that it has to make only these few presuppositions about human nature.

This view is foreign to the Jewish and Christian understanding of man as it can be found in their holy texts. Jewish thinking, especially, was originally far more holistic or collectivist. This could be exemplified from my own study of the justification for private property from classical antiquity to modern times.[4] In Christian ethics, the obvious point of departure was the conviction that the earth belonged to mankind collectively, whereas private property needed justification. The Fathers of the Church found such justification in different ways.

The natural rights theorists of the seventeenth century (Catholic and Protestant) found a sophisticated justification of private property, which took its point of departure in the doctrine of the "suum." In the view of Hugo Grotius, man had a personal sphere, his "suum," which was immune to infringement and violations by other human beings. The natural right to his "suum" could, however, be extended to external things.[5] This was to become the core of John Locke's justification of private property. By working on raw material, man impressed the material with his labor, skill, and creative imagination. So he extended his personal sphere to the object and made it his own.

I am well aware that the standard view is that, to Locke, the surplus value of man's work on an object is seen as his justification for the property right. But I am prepared to defend my own interpretation presented in my doctoral dissertation from 1977 (an interpretation inspired by the Swedish jurist Karl Olivecrona).

This view of man's relationship to external things has interesting implications. It is a cornerstone of liberal philosophy by virtue of its justification of private property. But, if I am right in my interpretation of Locke, this justification presupposes a more personal relationship to the work and its object than the interpretation according to which the justification is due to the abstract surplus value that is created by the work. Certainly there has been a shift from the ideal of the classical industrialist to the admired modern stockbroker. The relation of the latter to the means of production can hardly be said to be a direct, personal one.

It is interesting to note that the idea from Grotius and other natural rights theorists is reflected in the ideas of the young Karl Marx. In his view, labor should ideally be an interaction between man and nature. By his labor, man is naturalized and nature is cultivated, and by this interaction man would grow. He would develop higher needs and also the means to meet them. But, according to Marx, in capitalist society the fruits of his labor are instead taken from the worker, and his salary is a meager compensation, just enough to keep the worker alive and working. In this idea of an ideal interaction between man and the external world, which has elements both from natural rights theory and romanticism, man is seen not as an isolated, atomistic being, but as a person in interaction with, and with a diffuse demarcation towards, the external world. Man has, so to speak, a sensual, interdependent, and open relation to nature.

The Norwegian social philosopher Dag Österberg has invented the term "sociomateria" for all the material things that carry meaning and that are impressed by human intentions.[6]

The deep human aspiration to leave one's mark on the external world might have a biological origin. Torsten Malmberg has pointed to the phenomenon of human territoriality. Man, as well as other animals, has territories. The original purpose in seeking to establish a territory is to have a secure place for nourishment and reproduction. Animals may have individual territories or—if they live in groups—common group-territories.[7] It is obvious that much human behavior has its origin in the striving for a territory. Just one example: In the new office building of Novartis in Täby, the architect has created a very flexible working-place. People move around and just plug in their computers where they find an empty desk. But very soon employees began to mark their favorite places. Soon photographs of family members and other small things appeared on the boards. It is tempting to interpret this as a kind of territorial behavior. Or think of all the ways of creating a territory of one's own at the beach.

Torsten Malmberg describes parallels between animal and human territoriality.[8] He stresses three basic needs that territoriality fulfills:

identity, privacy, and safety. According to Malmberg the struggle for survival is first and foremost a struggle for space, and in the modern city the need for space is difficult to satisfy, and this fact causes psychic stress.[9] In a study, architect Christina Redvall refers to interviews that reflect the need for a territory.[10] For example: "It's about safety, isn't it? You have your little home where you can huddle up and be left in peace. Shut the door. A firm footing. It's safety, isn't it?" or "It is absolutely vital to belong somewhere. To feel that this is mine. That I can shut the door behind me."

We presume that animals try to defend a territory of their own that is large enough for nourishment and reproduction but small enough to be defended. Do human beings seek a territory, for example, a home, a garden, or a working-place, which is as large as possible? Is there an optimal size for a human territory? Perhaps there is one period in life for growing expectations, and another at the end of life for diminishing or concentrating the "life-space"? Could it be compared with a tendency of the severely ill to contract and concentrate bodily resources?

Let me sum up the view of man—the anthropology that follows from my observations so far. Man lives in interaction with and interdependence on the external material world, and the border between himself and that world is diffuse. This diffuse border delineates three concentric spheres: (1) the intimate sphere, (2) the social sphere, and (3) the territorial sphere.

The intimate sphere is typically constituted by the living body, but also by personal belongings, such as glasses, clothes, hearing-aid, rings, and so on. The intimate sphere is granted very strong legal protection. For instance, theft, which is combined with threat or violence against this sphere, is looked upon as especially encumbering.

The social sphere may consist of a person's nearest surroundings. First and foremost his home belongs to this category, but so may, for example, the car, or the writing desk, or else the working place. It is essential to note that the limits of this sphere may or may not coincide with the limits of his or her possessions. The law grants this sphere strong protection. Violation of the privacy of my home is a criminal offense, irrespective of whether it is linked to theft or other violations. Typically, it makes no difference (legally or morally) whether the home is owned or hired.

The territorial sphere may be much wider. It may include a big farm with many acres of land, or a village, or a town, or even a region or country. In Swedish, the term "hembygd" (English: "home district") signals a kinship with the word for the concept of a home (Swedish: "hem").

I will focus on the second and the third kinds of personal spheres.

The Home

The concept of a home is a wide concept. It has a rich content that is factual, emotive, and evaluative.[11] The English language does not have the more neutral term for it as has the German ("Wohnung") or the Swedish ("bostad"). In German there are two words that carry the same meaning as the English "home" (beside the more neutral "Wohnung"): "Heim," and compounds with "Haus"—zu Hause sein, etc. "Home," "Heim," and "Hem" all have strong positive connotations. This is notable if one considers that the home is often a place of conflicts and of sorrow. Most cases of violence against women and children are committed at home. These terms can be used for an individual home, but also in connection with greater territorial entities, such as *homeland, Heimat, hemland,* or *hemort.* There are related words that confer the idea of being at home as an ideal state: *homesick, Heimweh, hemlängtan, hemkänsla,* and others. To feel at home is obviously something positive.

In Swedish, the word has been used for political purposes in the catchword "folkhem," meaning a state where every citizen is treated as an equal family member. In Swedish there are examples of less successful attempts to make use of the positive charge of the term, for instance, in expressions like "barnhem," "ålderdomshem," or "sjukhem," which have been used euphemistically for institutions rather different from a home in the normal sense.

The specific activities for which a home serves are culturally bound, although the two earlier-mentioned functions of animal territoriality may be common—nourishment and reproduction. To put it plainly: eating and intercourse. Parallel to the professionalization of many of the functions of the family, the home has lost many of its earlier functions. In the old, traditional peasant society the home was a main working-place for an extended family. Schools and nursing homes have taken over much of the education and care giving today. Most of the day is spent outside the home.

Still, the patterns for designing a home are often taken from old forms of living. It is sometimes said that the red farmer-cottage is the dream and ideal of urban Swedish people today. At least it is easy to find patterns and ideals of that kind in modern architecture and interior decoration. You may find luxury villas built for several millions of Swedish crowns which have no dining room but a huge kitchen with plenty of space for dining. The count, the civil servant, and the clergyman in centuries past did have dining rooms, but the farmer did not. Today even wealthy people choose their ideals among the four classes of the past—at least partly from the farmers. In the farmhouse the kitchen was central. From the kitchen the house was heated; there the fireplace was situated. Consequently, the kitchen was a warm and cozy room (perhaps the only one). Furthermore, the kitchen represented food and communion, as hospitality has always been connected with eating. The Swedish saying "Egen härd är guld värd" (your own hearth is worth gold) implies that having your own fireplace, and thereby being able both to care for (giving shelter and warmth and food) yourself and for your guest, is a very precious thing.

When my mother was old and suffered from dementia, the kitchen, and especially the stove, became a great problem. This is not an unusual situation, and there are many smart devices for solving such problems. A good home for an elderly person would be a home without a stove. But this is almost unthinkable. I once discussed this matter with Bengt Lindqvist, former vice minister for health in Sweden. And I could not persuade him that homes for the elderly did not need a kitchen and a stove in every suite. The hearth of the house has a strongly symbolic meaning that is much more important than its practical utility.

Three different homes: The first home is the home of one's childhood. This is an extremely important place. It is the place from which the most basic impressions and experiences stem, for example, early learning concerning eating, personal hygiene, and social norms. The second home is the home built for oneself and one's family. This is the home where the head of the household is the king (or the queen), i.e. "My home is my castle." The third home is the home where a person is cared for when s/he gets ill or very old. In the first and third homes one has only limited sovereignty. In the second home the head of the household sets the rules and forms the rituals (even if there might be important differences between the sexes). It goes without saying that several people during their lifetimes may live in several homes of each category. Many also have an extra home for summer or winter vacations. For most people it is believed to be important to have a certain degree of continuity between consecutive homes. Some people will never live in the third home. For them the second home will be their last one. This was the case in my own family. My father and brother never had to move to a third home. And recently I have visited a summer neighbor during the last days of his life in his own home.

The relation between the three homes may cause problems. A home typically has other functions than being a place for medical care and attendance. The standard functions of a home hardly meet the requirements of a good place for care and attendance. When medical care is given both in the second and third homes, these needs and functions may conflict.

Home District

A home district is something that constitutes the largest area of the identity of a person. The German and the Scandinavian languages have better terms for a person's home district or native place. We speak of "hembygd" or "Heimat."

Coming home is definitely a cherished thing. To love one's home and to love one's home country are even moral ideals. A poor appreciation of one's home and country are usually looked upon with suspicion. Yi-Fu Tuan writes about "topophilia"—love for a place.[12] Torsten Malmberg emphasizes that deep relationships to places are as characteristic and necessary for human beings as are such relationships to people.[13]

The Norwegian philosopher Jakob Melöe has taken an interest in the concept of a place.[14] He has investigated the meaning of places (Norwegian: "steder") and the problem of how to delimit them. Unfortunately, he has written very little about this concept. A place, to Melöe, is a socio-economic as well as natural entity; it is an inhibited landscape so to speak. Ethical action, and human action in general, can only be rightly understood in its place-context. It is always rooted in a certain place.

How can a place be defined and delimited? Geographer Gerhard Gustafsson can help answer that question. He distinguishes three aspects of a landscape. First, there is the *pictorial landscape*, i.e. the momentarily-seen landscape. Second is the *perception landscape*. Here a broader time dimension is included. The landscape is experienced for some time, and it is experienced not only by sight but also by the other senses. Third, there is the *identification landscape*. "We might say that a 'symbolic landscape' has crystallized out after a long period of time."[15] The identification can be seen as the saturation of meaning (historical, practical, and symbolic) in the place or landscape.

Even art and literature play a role in the identification of the pictorial and the perception landscape. For instance, the pastoral landscape was "invented" by painters (and poets), not by farmers. The "wild" landscape was probably a product of early romanticism. For one account of the historic roots of this theme, see *The World is a Garden*, by Ilva Beretta.[16]

How does the appropriation of or identification with a home district come about? It is a process on several levels. I have mentioned the sensual, physical, appropriation attained by working on a raw material or cultivating a piece of nature. It can also be attained by incorporating an object into one's history by acquiring it in a special way, making it remind you of something important. Normally the home is the largest and most important artifact one produces during ones lifetime. In this process things and persons cannot easily be distinguished, because they acquire their meaning in narratives, i.e. in consistent wholes of symbolic meaning. On higher levels, scenery, landscapes, cities, regions can be appropriated by the senses as well as symbolically and historically. Once again: identification is attained by aesthetic means (direct experiences and works of art) and by incorporation into narratives, i.e. in this case, myth, legend, and history.

A bold endeavor at connecting the rich and positive concept of a home with the equally comprehensive concept of a state or nation into the metaphor of a national home (Swedish: "folkhem") was made in the early inter-war period in Sweden. Conservatives and nationalists like Axel Brusewitz and Rudolf Kjellén coined the term "folkhem," and later, during the 1940s, it was used by the social democratic prime minister Per Albin Hansson. The term was intended to encourage a feeling of kinship and solidarity, uniting all social classes in society. Until recently the ideal of a "folkhem" played an important role in the building of the Swedish welfare state.[17]

Even more interesting for the historical understanding of the significance of the home district is the movement for small-holdings (Swedish: "egnahemsrörelsen"). As an answer to the extensive emigration (first and foremost to North America) during the late nineteenth century, caused by poverty, destitution, and social marginalization (for instance of religious dissidents), the government launched a program for providing favorable loans to those who wanted to build small self-supporting farms. This movement later included cheap long-term loans for building small family-houses even in cities and villages. The aim of this movement could simply be described as an effort to facilitate for people the planting of roots in their society.

I have assumed that a home district can be appropriated and identified with on many levels, and that it therefore can have different extensions. Former Swedish prime minister Carl Bildt described himself, in the title of an autobiographical book, as "hallänning, svensk och europé" (being from the province of Halland, being a Swede and being a European). Thus he described his home district as concentric. I take it that this kind of identification is common. Some people would include even smaller and also greater areas in their identity; let us say a small village in Halland and a feeling of belonging to the "global village." But it is interesting to note that other people might describe their identity as rather "bicentric" or "multi-centric." For my own part, I might describe my identity in that way. I was born in the province of Skåne, where I grew up and began my studies. I have my summerhouse there and often stay there even in wintertime (I could easily be identified by my dialect as coming from that part of Sweden). But I have lived most of my life in Uppsala in the middle of Sweden. My daughters have included South Africa, Great Britain, and the USA respectively in their identity by having lived and worked there, and by the fact that their boyfriends come from these countries.

I have described rootedness in places as corresponding to deep human needs. Man's territoriality is deeply rooted. But I do not want to give the impression that territoriality and rootedness is always something positive and uncontroversial. It may suffice to think of the jargon of "Blut und Boden" and of thousands of controversies about borders and ground. It must also be said that the supposed fact that territoriality has biological roots does not mean that it is thereby morally justified. It should also be remembered that millions of people today are displaced, that they have neither a home nor a home district: they are literally homeless.

The justification of a home or a home district depends upon whether it furthers the aforementioned three goods (which, according to Malmberg, also correspond to the three basic territorial needs), namely security, autonomy, and identity. Security and autonomy are, to my mind, self-evident moral goods. That identity—the need to express oneself in the external world by leaving one's mark upon it, working on it, and thereby appropriating it—is a genuine and legitimate human need, I hope I have demonstrated.

Let me finally cite Torsten Malmberg at some length: "To have roots in a place is to possess a secure base, from which to look out over the world, a firm grasp of one's own position in the order of things. Deep relationships with places is as necessary and perhaps as unavoidable as similar ones with people. Without such relations human existence, while possible, is bereft of much significance."[18]

Notes

1. Weil, 1978.
2. Lantz, 2000.
3. Möller, 1998.
4. Lantz, 1977.
5. Grotius, 1701; Olivecrona, 1969 & 1974, and Lantz, 1977.
6. Österberg, 1977.
7. Malmberg, 1980 & 1983.
8. Malmberg, 1980.
9. Malmberg, 1983, p 135.
10. Redvall, 1987.
11. Lantz, 1996.
12. Tuan, 1974.
13. Malmberg, 1986.
14. Melöe, 1993a & 1993b.
15. Gustafsson, 1991, p. 29.
16. Beretta, 1993.
17. Lagergren, 1999.
18. Malmberg, 1980.

2

Reverence, Respect, and Dependence

Paul Woodruff

Introductory

We are, if we wish to be, beneficiaries of two ancient traditions that developed elaborate theories of virtues—elements of character that enable individuals to flourish in communities. The ancient Greek tradition began with Homer and passed through later poets into the hands of philosophers, was well developed in the work of Aristotle, and continued in Hellenistic ethics.[1] The ancient Chinese tradition was already in place when Confucius became its central teacher, reached a mature stage with Mencius, and continued through many periods to a high point in the Ming Dynasty.[2]

The ancient Greek poets celebrated two clusters of virtues that were widely believed to be essential to the survival of human communities, and therefore to the survival of the species. One cluster centers on *Themis* (Right) and *Nemesis* (Just deserts) and falls in classical times entirely under *Dike* or *Dikaiosune* (Justice). The other cluster centers on *Aidos* (Reverence or Shame); to this belongs the closely related pair *Eusebeia* (Good respect or Piety) and *Hosiotes* (Holiness or Piety), as well as their consequences *Sophrosune* (Soundmindedness) and *Euboulia* (Good judgment). For simplicity, I shall call the first cluster justice, and the second reverence.[3]

Plato held that the reverence is the part of justice that governs human relations with the gods; he therefore seems to have treated justice, but not reverence, as one of the primary virtues.[4] Reverence was of utmost importance, however, to the tragic poets, whose authority on ethics he vehemently rejected. Justice has therefore been much discussed by philosophers; reverence has not.

The poets understood the two clusters to be complementary, governing different kinds of situations (but with some overlap). Justice is at issue mainly between equals who can present themselves to a judge or a king and request that a just decision be made between them.[5] Reverence is at issue mainly between unequals; it holds back the hand of power from wanton abuse of the helpless, and through fear of shame it leads strong people to act well even when there is no one stronger to bring them to justice. Reverence is the virtue that is absent from the rulers that the ancient Greeks called tyrants. The tragic poets made the absence of reverence conspicuous in stage tyrants such as Pentheus and Creon.

Creon is a useful example: In the *Antigone* of Sophocles, Creon decides to withhold burial from his rebel nephew, who has died in attacking the city-state. Creon thinks this is what Justice requires; he is aware of only one sort of Reverence, and that is the respect he believes is due to him as king. His failures of Reverence are many, and they result in disastrously bad judgment.

Human duties to the dead flow from Reverence, not Justice. Reverence, moreover, requires that a ruler pay attention to the opinions of his subjects, but Creon treats most of those who speak to him with contempt. He tries to bully the Watchman and falsely assumes the worst of him, as he does of most of the other characters: he thinks that the loyal Ismene is guilty, that the prophet Tiresias has been bribed, and that his own son is a woman's toy. Because he is unwilling to take advice, he goes off course and brings destruction on his own head.

Any story in which a tyrant falls would have been delightful to audiences in democratic, tyrant-hating Athens. They would have agreed with the poet as to why a tyrant goes wrong: the tyrant's failure is irreverence. Plato, as is well known, had a different diagnosis—and a far less democratic one. He thought that the primary fault of a tyrant was injustice. Justice does not require that a ruler pay attention to the ignorant rabble, and Plato's philosopher kings would have no respect for the opinions of the people they rule. But in ancient Athens, any citizen had a right to speak. And wherever Reverence is observed, (the Athenians believed) leaders will respect what their followers say.

In this essay my main topic will be respect. I will take Reverence to be the virtue that governs the balance between respect and contempt—just as I take Courage to be the virtue that governs the balance between fear and confidence. There is a time for respect, and a time for contempt; part of being reverent is coming to those different times with the feelings that are right for each.

Reverence: A Preview

This is not a matter of religion. Classical reverence is a virtue of community that may or may not be exercised in a religious context. It has a major place in the secular ethics of Confucianism, and it was important to a number of thinkers in ancient Greece who were agnostic about the gods—thinkers who would fit a modern definition of humanism (Protagoras and Thucydides).

Because reverence is neutral with respect to religion,[6] it can be cultivated in a multicultural and multireligious community—perhaps even a global one—and we can reasonably hope for an overlapping consensus on its value. Indeed, when members of different religions admire each other's virtues, what they admire is primarily reverence, since they cannot be giving approval to the beliefs and practices of an alien religion as such. They can, however, approve of the virtuous manner in which the practices are followed. And that is reverence.

Reverence is easily misunderstood and has been submerged in both traditions. In the Greek tradition, reverence was overshadowed by justice, as we have seen. In the Chinese tradition, reverence was overshadowed by ceremony. The same word (*Li*) is used for both ceremony and the virtue that is expressed in ceremony; but it is easier to keep up the ceremonies than it is to cultivate the virtue, and emphasis shifted toward ceremony even in classical writers other than Mencius.

In the Greek tradition, the main element in reverence is the recognition that one is neither a god nor a wild beast—accepting on the one hand that one is neither infallible nor immortal, and on the other that one must observe certain ceremonies (burying the dead, for example). Failures show the same double pattern. We have already seen how irreverent rulers may carry on as if they knew as much as gods, listening to no one's advice. On the other side of the coin, irreverent heroes may carry on like wild beasts, living in rough huts on a beach with captured women and exposing their human kills to carrion dogs and birds (Achilles). The reverent hero, by contrast, lives in a home with a family (Hector).

Reverence was a factor in Homer, but it was most celebrated by the tragic poets. Their ethical views influenced the historians

Herodotus and Thucydides, and perhaps also the teacher Protagoras. Herodotus illustrated reverence and its failures in several anecdotes; Thucydides saw reverence as one of the main casualties of civil war and therefore, by implication, a source of stability in a *polis* (city-state).

Protagoras (apparently) represented reverence and justice as the two virtues that are absolutely necessary to any stable human association; he indicated through a myth that the capacity to acquire these virtues is universal in human beings who are not defective, and that these virtues are developed first through training in early childhood and later through formal education such as he provided. He emphasized the importance of good judgment (*euboulia*), the virtue of thought that enables one, in the absence of the relevant knowledge, to make reasonable decisions (probably through consultation and the weighing of defeasible arguments on both sides for alternative courses of action).[7]

Plato had no interest in *euboulia*, because he did not believe there could be a virtue of thought in the absence of knowledge. Unlike the poets and sophists, Plato apparently did not think it a virtue to abandon the search for infallible knowledge. Plato therefore rejected the ethical outlook of the poets entirely. Aristotle, though he liked the poets, did nothing to revive their ethical views. Plato treated reverence as a mere part of justice and in his mature work omitted it from his list of virtues (though he left a place for its expression in his ideal cities).[8] Reverence does not play a role in Aristotle's ethics, although his theory of virtue accommodates very well to reverence, as we shall see. The result is that I am able to draw on the two great philosophers for a theory of virtue, but not for an account of reverence.

Virtues of Character

The following sketch of a theory of virtues of character is based mainly on ancient Greek models, heavily influenced by Aristotle.[9]

1 A virtue is an element in a person's character that tempers emotions at the source.

The principal virtues of character, for the purpose of this essay, are courage, fairmindedness, compassion, and reverence. I shall not discuss here the cognitive virtues, such as mindfulness. But keep in mind that you cannot exercise any of the virtues of character without being mindful both of your circumstances and of what it is that you are doing.[10] I shall also pass over the main objections to virtue ethics, which are two: (1) That virtue ethics presupposes a view of character that we now know to be false.[11] (2) That virtue ethics leads to relativism, because conceptions of virtue are embedded in cultures.[12]

A virtue is the capacity, partly natural and partly cultivated, to experience the right emotions at the right time and at the right level in each circumstance. Simply, a virtue is what makes you feel like doing the right thing. If you have the virtue that tempers fear and confidence, for example, then you experience fear and confidence at the optimum level for each circumstance. And that is called courage. It is a different sort of thing from the ability you might have to control excessive fear and confidence after they come upon you.

Self-control is not a virtue in this account; it is, rather, something you may be able to fall back on if virtue fails you. But self-control is a weak fallback, because emotions are very powerfully motivating. This part of my account has three important consequences for our discussion:

1.1 Virtues are internal. Virtues are part of the motivational system of the person who has them. There is no need to ask the question, "Why should I do the thing that is courageous?" If you are courageous, you will want to do that thing.

"Internal" is a figure of speech with some unfortunate connotations. The theory does not presuppose a monolithic self in which courage inheres; it is consistent with any of a variety of theories that would allow us to say, in the case of courage, that part of you wants to do the courageous thing, and part does not. The highest degree of courage, however, will be in the person who is courageous all through (and so with the other virtues).

1.11 Virtues sustain both individuals and communities. There is a good reason to ask: "Why should I cultivate in myself and my children the virtue of courage?" And this allows a very simple answer— "Because people who have courage are less likely to be disabled by excessive fear and less likely to be swayed by overconfidence to take risks that will lead to their destruction." If you have courage, you will be more likely on the whole to live longer, and do more of the things that you want, than if you do not have courage. If courage were fearlessness, this would not be so, because fearlessness may well lead to early death. But courage has survival value, if not for the individual, at least for the community. Any of the principal virtues—courage, fairmindedness, compassion, and reverence—might lead to self-sacrifice of a sort that is beneficial to the community and is, therefore, in the interests of the individual broadly construed.[13]

Imagine a fishing village without the courage that in real villages sustains both the fishermen and their families by helping them maintain the right level of confidence for their circumstances. In the imaginary village without courage, the fishermen would either drown through taking foolish risks, or starve their families by taking no risks at all, while their families would either urge them into voyages that are too dangerous or keep them from going to sea.

For a more believable case, imagine a community in which the sense of fairmindedness had been stamped out by sustained outrages against justice, carried out by or under the protection of a ruthless, illegitimate police force. Now imagine the police suddenly removed. What is there remaining in the community that could stave off violent anarchy?[14]

1.2 Virtues are natural. Virtues are natural in three ways. They govern emotions that are natural for us to have, such as fear, and they govern them in ways that help us satisfy needs that are ours by nature, such as the need to do well in circumstances evoking fear. Our ability to acquire virtues is evidence that we are, by nature, able to do so. If virtues are natural, then they can be recognized and admired and cultivated across cultural barriers—a possibility that brings with it opportunities for global conversations on ethics.

As a human good, courage is similar to physical health, and we may reasonably suppose that every normal human being is born with the potential for courage, just as everyone who is normal is born with the potential for good physical health. The criterion for "normal" in this discussion must be a continually revised hypothesis about human nature based on ongoing studies of the capacities of human beings.

Modern philosophers have dug a famous pitfall for naturalistic ethics. The open-question argument is supposed to show that ethical conclusions require ethical premises. You cannot derive from the "is"-type statement, "you made a promise," the "ought"-type conclusion, "you ought to keep that promise," because it is still open for you to ask *why* you ought to keep the promise—though this would be a strange question from someone who knows enough about what promises mean that s/he could seriously make one.

This trap does not catch virtue—at least not in the same way. A health analogy is instructive. If, when you take your child to a doctor, the doctor tells you that certain measures will promote health, the following question is open in the philosopher's sense, but no sane person would ask it: "But why ought I to wish that my child be in health?" If this question were a reality for you, you would not have visited the doctor in the first place.

Part of the task of virtue ethics is to show that the analogy between virtue and health is strong enough to carry virtue across such pitfalls as the naturalistic fallacy. That is the task Plato takes up in the *Republic* in the case of justice. Justice is a much harder case than courage. As I have sketched an account of courage, courage is very much like health; but justice, as the ancient Greeks knew it, is mainly a matter of not taking more than my fair share in relation to other people. And it is not easy to see why other people should have any place in an account of my own health of character.

The case is easier for fairmindedness, and this, I would argue, is the virtue to defend, because it includes a sense of justice. I have already given an example to suggest how fairmindedness sustains community. It sustains individuals as well. Fairmindedness is shown in anger or outrage at injustice; individuals who entirely lack the ability to be angered by wrongs done to them will not be moved to stand up for their own interests. Individuals who are excessively angered by perceived wrongs will not be able to make the compromises they must make in order to find places for themselves in society (which itself is a natural need). So you must have fairmindedness in regard to yourself, and you will surely want to cultivate it in your children. And such a person will most likely be fairminded in regard to others as well. An important feature of virtues is that they are not readily dammed up; if you can be angered by wrongs done to you, you can be angered by wrongs done to other people. So a broad fairmindedness is a kind of health of character.

1.3 Virtues are cultural. Here the analogy with health breaks down. Health is the same for all human beings; any virtue, however, is embedded in the cultural practices in which it is expressed. Optimum levels of fear and confidence, for example, may be set differently for different practices (fishing may require more confidence than hunting, for example), and different cultures engage in different practices. Even within the same practices, virtues may be expressed differently in different cultures, and differently even within one culture for different groups (say, for men and women).[15]

How, one asks, can virtues be both natural and cultural? Many human phenomena are both natural and cultural. It is natural for humans to learn a language, but there is no one language that it is natural to learn. In the same way, it may be natural to cultivate virtue, but there is no one system of virtue that it is natural to cultivate.

There are two distinctions to keep in mind:

1.31 Truth and opinion. Opinions may vary widely as to what are the optimum levels of fear and confidence, but the truth may turn out to be the same for all. I suspect, however, that the answer is much more complicated, because we are talking about optimum levels for each circumstance, and different people face different circumstances. Ideally, courage would allow you to adapt to many different circumstances, but the norms laid down in your culture are probably aimed at selected circumstances only. So when your culture declares norms for courage, these norms cannot define all of courage. Treat any culturally embedded definition of virtue as a partial account of the whole. (Plato would say that courage as your culture perceives it *participates* in courage as it really is, which is the courage none of us really knows.)

1.32 Virtue and its expression. Cultures differ as to whether a courageous person may reveal the fears that she quite rightly feels. The expression of virtuous emotions involves different languages of behavior in different cultures. One should not suppose, because a people have no words for fear or courage, that they have no fear or courage.

1.4 Virtues involve choice but are not entirely up to the individual. Neither acquiring virtue nor acting from virtue is the direct result of free choice. Indeed, there are elements of both choice and good fortune in virtue. No one can take full credit for being virtuous or full blame for being vicious.

1.41 Such choices as do occur may not be rational. In order to act courageously, you must act from courage, but not necessarily on the basis of a rational choice to do so in each case. Situations that call for courage rarely give time for rational choice, and so it is with many virtues. Your history of prior choices, however, sets a general course that you will be likely to follow without thinking.

1.42 Virtue depends on natural capacity. Insofar as a virtue depends on a natural capacity, you cannot simply choose to have a virtue any more than you can simply choose to have good health. If you are born with a congenital anemia, you are unlucky. If you are born with a tendency to be overwhelmed by fear, you are equally unlucky. You may, however, make choices that will improve your health or destroy it.

1.43 You do not choose your surrounding culture. And yet this determines the language of behavior in which your virtues or vices will be expressed. You do, however, retain a certain range of cultural choice through association and friendship—by joining, or not joining, certain groups.

1.44 You do not choose those who care for you in early childhood. Even so, they will have a large effect on how you develop your capacities for virtue. Again, you have some measure of choice— e.g. you may choose your friends.

Reverence

2 Reverence is the virtuous capacity for awe, respect, and shame.

These three feelings are associated with reverence in both ancient Greek and ancient Chinese traditions, and they all belong to the affective side of what we might call "knowing your place" as a human being. Irreverence, for the Greeks, is forgetting that you are mortal and trying to play the part of a god; this is the main ethical theme of ancient Greek tragedy: that the virtue which wards off *hubris* is reverence.

In the Confucian tradition, personal gods have no place. The Confucian analog to hubris is for an ordinary ruler to take on the prerogatives of the Emperor, the Son of Heaven. There was no Emperor in the time of Confucius, only rulers of warring states, and so the Emperor in his system has something of the ideal status of a philosopher king in Plato's.[16] (The philosopher king in Plato's system does have divine attributes, by the way; Plato does not entirely support the poets' conception of reverence.)

2.1 Awe is for something that reminds us of human limitations. And this "something" is the object of reverence. We speak of reverence to God, to nature, and to ideals such as justice and truth. A scientist who is reverent towards the truth is reverent in seeking the truth. Her very reverence makes her cautious; it prevents her from saying that she knows exactly what the truth is and keeps her mind open to evidence that may make her adjust her theory.

There are four conditions for an object of reverence (OR); only the first is essential:

2.11 OR cannot be changed or controlled by human means.

2.12 OR is not fully understood by human experts.

2.13 OR was not created by human beings.

2.14 OR transcends cultural boundaries.

Certain works of art may also be thought to be out of our control in a relevant way. For a reverent scientist, the OR could be the final explanation for the universe, which satisfies the first and third conditions. For a reverent statesperson, the OR might be justice, conceived as an ideal, dimly grasped and much disputed, by which we should try to regulate our poor systems of law. This might satisfy all four conditions. For religious naturalists, OR would be nature, or the universe. For many people, the OR will be conceived as divine.

To say that I am reverent towards X does not imply that I think that X is spooky (the truth is not spooky to a scientist); but a claim of reverence does usually imply that I recognize that X is not entirely under my control, that I think X is what it is no matter what I do or believe, and that I accept a degree of mystery about X which I am trying to penetrate. Reverent believers in God do not pretend to know exactly what is in the mind of God, and they do not attempt to speak literally the mind of God. That is why reverent believers are not fundamentalists.

Reverence is often silent or inarticulate (unlike faith, which is often noisy and may be clearly defined by a creed). This is why it is primarily expressed in ceremony, as we shall see, and this is why it is essential to wordless forms of art such as music and dance, or to the divided articulation of theater.

2.2 Respect is for those who share certain practices expressing reverence. Reverence helps us to avoid treating other human beings with contempt, partly because it reminds us of our limitations, and partly because it can be shared in a variety of practices. The ceremonial aspect of a scholarly conference, for example, expresses a common reverence for the truth that is sought, and those who share this reverence respect one another.

2.21 Respect is mutual. Students will not respect a teacher who treats them with contempt, and vice versa.

2.22 Respect is expressed in ceremony. In the classroom, for example, teacher and students show mutual respect by observing certain rules—not interrupting, waiting to speak until called upon, etc. These rules (by my account) define classroom ceremony, which expresses at the same time mutual respect and shared reverence.[17]

We shall see that respect is too thin when it is accorded to everyone, whether they respond to it or not, and it is too thick when it waits upon considered judgments of other people's qualities. Reverence lies on a mean in relation to respect, neither too thin nor too thick. Thick respect fails, because useful respect is not a product of judgment. That is, we do not wait until we have reason to judge that our students are capable before we treat them with respect. We must treat them with respect from the outset, if we are to have an opportunity to judge their capabilities fairly. Thin respect fails, because useful respect can be withdrawn, or not offered, if circumstances warrant. Respect is wasted on those who do not return it, for example. Universal respect, like universal love, would not take into consideration the variety of relationships that are essential to community.[18]

2.3 Shame is for exposure as falling short. Without reverence, we may feel shame as pain on being exposed to other people for having violated community standards—and this is not a virtuous response, because you may be in the right. Shame without reverence undermines autonomy. For this reason, rationalist critics in the ancient world tried to downplay shame as a source of motivation. But shame cannot be eliminated: it is among the most powerful human motivators (along with fear, love, and anger), and it appears to be ours by nature.

When reverence is in play, we feel shame when exposed in our own minds to shortcomings vis-à-vis the ideals towards which we stand in awe, and this reaction does belong to virtue.

The ancient Greeks used the same word, *aidos*, for shame, reverence, and awe, as if these were the same things. But it cannot be exactly the same to feel a sense of awe at the majesty of God's knowledge, and to be ashamed of being wrong on a particular point (although these are related). You cannot reasonably try to be infallible, and you should not be ashamed at being fallible; but you can try to avoid making mistakes, and in some cases you should be ashamed of the mistakes you have made.

2.4 Ceremony is the expression of reverence. Without reverence, ceremony is empty. Because modern thinkers have lost sight of reverence as a virtue, they tend to think of ceremony as intrinsically empty. But it is not. The value of ceremony is threefold.

2.41 Ceremony constrains leaders. If rulers accept ceremony as limiting their freedom of action, they have already-set limits to their power. If they do so out of reverence for something that transcends human efforts (God, Heaven, Justice or Law conceived as an ideal and not simply a human product, Nature, etc.), those limits are a real check on the ruler's power, and they are internal to the character of the ruler. In any system of power (democratic or otherwise) there are people whose power is such that it can be limited only by their own virtues. Nothing could otherwise hold such people back.

2.42 Ceremony expresses shared reverence. If the object of your reverence satisfies all of the conditions I have proposed, it will ultimately be mysterious, and you will then not be able to express your reverence outside of ceremony. Part of the beauty of ceremony is that it is often inarticulate. Keep in mind that you cannot have ceremonies all by yourself, any more than you can have a language all by yourself. Reverence requires community.

2.43 Reverence makes community possible. Ceremony enables groups of people to function as communities based on mutual respect. Meetings are ceremonies; so are conferences and classes, sporting events, and artistic performances. In meetings, ceremony enables a group to feel a sense of unity even when they disagree about specifics.[19]

3 Individuals and Community

Courage is like health: a reasonable person can easily see how it is in his interests as an individual to cultivate courage in himself and in those he loves. It seems, like health, to be primarily a quality of individuals. Reverence, by contrast, is a virtue that belongs to people in communities—in the home, in families, and in the state. If you lack reverence, according to the theory I have sketched above, you would not function well in a community. This brings us to the big question: Why should you care about having the virtues of community?

First, a corrective about courage (and also about health): It only *seems* that courage is a virtue of individuals. In fact, the matter is complex. To cultivate a virtue, you must have opportunities to express it in action, but you will find fewer opportunities for virtue if you are not in a virtuous community. Imagine that you are at war and find yourself in a unit of cowards. None of them is willing to take the slightest risk. You could go on by yourself and throw away your life, but that is foolish and not courageous. By yourself, you may not be able to find anything courageous to do. What could a brave man do in occupied Norway or France if it was impossible to form a resistance group? Courage would have no outlet.

Generally, the virtues of individuals depend on the virtues of their communities, both because virtue-acquisition from early childhood depends heavily on examples and because the expression of virtue in action frequently depends on the virtues of the community. In the last analysis, all virtues are virtues of community: We acquire them in a community, and we practice them in a community. But this is especially clear in the case of reverence.

It is not easy to show reverence in an irreverent society. "Virtue has neighbors," says Confucius (*Analects* 4.25), and virtue never works as it is supposed to work in a vacuum or in a hostile human environment. We saw that the social factor is important for courage; it is even more important for reverence, which typically affects the shared behavior and shared feelings of people in a group.

4 Respect and Dependence

Respect would appear to be a hard case for the claim that the exercise of virtue is dependent on the presence of virtue in the community. If the dependence claim is right, then I could not treat you with respect outside of a certain kind of social milieu. But why should my respect for you depend on anything but the two of us?

Under the influence of Kant, we tend to think of respect as a recognition of autonomy: if you and I enjoy mutual respect, we are appreciating each other's autonomy. But "autonomy" can be used as a synonym for "independence," and this cannot be the sense of autonomy we want. Independence is not a human good—not, at least, if it means not depending on other people, or not depending on other people's judgments. Virtue does depend. We must find another way to understand autonomy if we wish to consider it among the human goods.

Consider the paradox of respect.[20] Because respect is mutual, leaders and teachers who wish to be respected must give respect to those beneath them. But why listen to people who know less than you do about the matter at hand?

Respect comes in three degrees of thickness: too thick, too thin, and just right. Thick respect is a judgment of quality, and is supposed to be due only to those who deserve it. Thin respect expresses only equality, and is due to every human being. But the respect that flows from reverence is a felt recognition of a connection growing out of common practices. You owe reverent respect to anyone who satisfies two conditions—he or she (1) belongs to a practice in common with you and (2) recognizes his or her position in the practice.

Let us begin with thick respect, which I am supposed to owe only to those who are better than others: I owe thick respect in sports to the better athlete, in class to the better student, and so forth. On this account, if I set out to teach you Greek but find that your Greek is better than mine, then I should both respect you and ask to become your student. But I never owe you thick respect for your knowledge of the subject unless you should be my teacher.

Thick respect cannot be all there is. Respect cannot follow upon judgments of quality, because judgments of quality must follow upon respect if they are to be fair. Suppose the issue is whether I should respect you for your wisdom in deciding to order the troops to re-treat. Then I must first respect you enough to take the time to exam-ine your reasons for giving the command. If I do not do so, my judgment of you will be unfair—either too stingy or too generous.

To make matters worse, if respect is only a judgment of quality, then I will never have a good reason to respect the opinions on a subject of anyone who has a good reason to be my student on that subject—because I would always know more than such a student. And my students—not knowing my subject—will have no good grounds for respecting me. They would have to master the subject before they could judge my work, and only then, on this theory, could they have reason to respect me. But how will they learn the subject if they do not respect their teacher? So it cannot be thick respect that develops between student and teacher, and we will keep our minds clear if we distinguish respect from judgment.

Thin respect is no more helpful in understanding teaching and leadership. It treats all human beings with respect because of their common humanity. In you I find the same capacities and the same weaknesses—the same mortality and the same desire to live—that I know in my own case, and so I treat you with thin respect. But who would care to earn and keep my respect if I offer it to everyone? In the richer, more usual use of the word, "respect" is for something that can be rightly given or withheld. Equality is a fine ideal, but it is fatal to a rich conception of respect, as Harry Frankfurt has shown.[21]

Moreover, we witness the failure of thin respect every day. Respect for people merely as human individuals has not been enough, in most cases, to overcome the catastrophic effects of differences in faith or nationality. For that we require more substantial connections, and thicker respect, such as grows in people who share a practice. When athletes of different backgrounds work together on a team, respect grows. But this is not thin respect, and it is not for everyone; it is for members of the team.

The respect that belongs to reverence, and expresses a moral character, is neither too thick nor too thin. It is a feeling that is built into special relationships. Your respect, if you are a leader, helps your followers feel that they belong in the group that you lead. Your contempt makes them feel left out, overlooked, irrelevant. To understand respect in a given society, you need to look closely at how groups work together in their culture.

Confucians develop respect in the family from early childhood. Family relationships, they believed, were undermined by the idea of universal love (due to Mo Tzu, a classical Chinese variety of egalitarianism).[22] In much the same vein, Aristotle complained against Plato. Plato had proposed (*Republic* 5) to make family love universal in the ideal city by replacing the nuclear family with a citywide family in which all men of the guardian class share all the women as wives and all youngsters as children. Aristotle thought Plato made more than a mistake in scale: Family and city are not just different sizes, they are different sorts of social entities altogether and require different sorts of ties among their members (*Politics* 2.3, 2.4). But the whole of humanity! What could it mean to show equal respect to everyone? Can universal respect be respect in the true sense?

The respect that is just right flows from shared reverence, and this reverence is *for* a common object of reverence. Instead of asking simply, "To whom is respect due?" we should ask, "What are the objects of reverence in a family, that allow the family members to cultivate mutual respect? What are they in a military unit? In a classroom? And how does this reverence determine when respect is rightly given, and when rightly denied?"

Respect is rightly given among those who revere the same object—for example, among teachers and students who treat learning with reverence. Respect is rightly taken away from those who violate the reverence of the group—for example, from students who treat learning with contempt. No teacher owes such a student respect in the classroom. This student refuses to be a member of the learning community, and it would be a lie to pretend otherwise. There may be other communities that teacher and student share, in terms of which they may share respect, but the classroom is not one of them. A good teacher will expel an irretrievably irreverent student from the classroom.

This need not be the end of the matter. A teacher who cares about whole people (and not just about people as students) would look for ways outside the classroom to build respect with the disruptive student. Music, theater, sports, even (where this is permitted) religion may save the youth from falling outside all circles of respect. That is one reason why such practices must be part of the education of young people. Without a wide range of respect-growing activities, some young people will not be able to be integrated into a community of respect.

Reverence in the family expresses a sense of family unity—that these people belong together, in the various roles assigned them under their culture, relative to the function of the family. In modern cultures, the function of the family is vastly diminished, and with it the importance of family ceremony and the internal system of respect that ceremony represents. All the more important, then, that families be able to share more than just being families by keeping alive music, sports, religion, or the like, in the home.

In a sports team or military unit, we easily see how respect is distributed and why. Soldiers and officers, players and coaches, respect each other insofar as they are serious in the way they approach their work, if they hold up their end, if they are not simply aiming for their own promotions—if, in other words, they work smoothly as parts of the team. They share a common goal, and in the best case they are passionate about it. Team spirit, patriotism, and, at the highest level, a passion for justice and peace—these are the feelings that allow respect to grow strong. Towards the end of the war in Vietnam, U.S. Army units showed a precipitous decline in respect for officers; this came in exact parallel with the loss of the idea that the aims of the war included such reverence-inspiring goals as peace or freedom or justice—just as the theory of respect-from-reverence would predict.

A reverent leader is devoted to ideals such as freedom and justice. A reverent leader need not pretend to be godlike; the ideals he or she reveres are godlike enough. Soldiers will not follow an officer who is clueless or who leads them into disaster. But in a healthy unit, soldiers can respect an officer who makes unfair or wrong decisions, if they recognize in that officer a commitment to fairness and the common good. They will actually respect their officers all the more if they do not catch them hiding their mistakes or blaming them on other people.

So it is in the classroom. Teachers and students can both go wrong—and be honest about it—without breaching mutual respect. Teachers can handle a totally ignorant class, but they face an impossible task if they are assigned a thoroughly irreverent gaggle, in which the desire to learn has been rooted out. That is just a roomful of students, not a class, and there is no basis for respect in being merely a roomful.

Reverent respect cannot grow just anywhere or for just anyone. What it needs in the classroom is not knowledge, which is always unevenly distributed, but the reverent desire for it, which can, at least in principle, be shared by all. That is the answer to the paradox of respect. What lies behind the teacher's respect for students is devotion to knowledge, and it is this that draws teacher and students into the circle of mutual respect. The conditions for respect depend not simply on individual character, but on community.

Notes

1. Aristotle's ethics are discussed, for example, in Sherman, 1989 and White, 1992; the broader tradition of ancient ethics is discussed in Annas, 1993.
2. For the Confucian tradition see Ivanhoe, 1999 and 2000.
3. For the pair *Aidos, Nemesis*, see Hesiod, *Works and Days* 197. For *Aidos, Dike*, see Protagoras in Plato's *Protagoras* 322c. For reverence in ancient Greek poetry and history, see Woodruff, 2001, pp. 81-101.
4. For Plato's treatment of reverence, see Woodruff, 2001, pp. 142-44, 229-30.
5. Thucydides 5.89, for example.
6. Woodruff, 2001, pp. 135-47.
7. Protagoras in Plato's *Protagoras* 322c (*Aidos* and *Dike*) and 319a (*Euboulia*). On the importance of the latter, see Woodruff, 1999.
8. See note 4 above.
9. The revival of interest in virtue ethics began with MacIntyre, 1981. Notable contributions are Pincoffs, 1986, Nussbaum, 1986, Thomas, 1989, O'Neil, 1996, and Crisp and Slote, 1997.
10. Goodenough and Woodruff, 2001.
11. Harman and some others object to the notion of character used by virtue ethics on the grounds that it has been refuted by such experiments as Milgram's famous experiment of 1963 (Harman, 2000, pp. 195-78). The objection is ill grounded; all ancient virtue theorists recognize that an individual's character depends radically on

community; that is why Aristotle's *Ethics* is to be read as embedded in his *Politics*. But the Milgram experiment substitutes for a virtue-supporting community one that has the results he reported.

12. Differences in culture are alleged to be grounds for another objection to virtue ethics (Kane, 1996, p. 223; cf. Harman's defense of relativism, 2000, pp. 3-99). Such an objection is to be answered partly by the refutation of relativism (Nussbaum, 1988; Okin, 1999; Woodruff, 2001, pp. 149-61) and partly by showing a natural basis for the broad similarities we find among cultures in respect of the principal virtues.

13. "Interests broadly construed": I take it that most people, without benefit of social philosophy, do not distinguish sharply between their personal interests and those of their children. From this it is a small step to the interests of the community that would sustain the children after the loss of the parents, and from this to a village and beyond.

14. Consider the example of segments of society in post-Soviet Russia.

15. See note 12 above.

16. Woodruff, 2001, pp. 103-15.

17. On the relation between virtues and rules, see Braybrooke, 1988.

18. See below, the section on "Respect and Dependence."

19. Kertzer, 1988 is helpful on the value of ritual in politics, especially in view of what he calls the ambiguity of ritual. See also Woodruff, 2001, pp. 19-22, 25-29.

20. This discussion of respect is drawn from Woodruff, 2001, pp. 197-203.

21. Frankfurt, 1999, on the subject of respect and community.

22. For an example of Confucian criticism of Mohist universalism, see Mencius 3 B 9: Universal love would imply no special respect for a king or father. But without special respect for a king or father you are in the condition of an animal.

3

Aesthetic Experience and Virtue: Narrative, Emotions, and the Understanding of Others

Katarina Elam

Introduction

In this paper, the purpose is to consider some aspects of the complex connection that seems to be found between emotions and narrative art. The main issue concerns in what sense emotions are a mode of understanding other human beings and art, and if this way of understanding can be communicated through fictional narratives. The emotion I shall concentrate on is compassion, although the discussion will have relevance for other emotions as well. It is the process of understanding the operation itself that is of primary interest. To imagine how someone else experiences his or her situation is to challenge one's self-centered perspective. To imagine the perspective of people from foreign cultures is furthermore to challenge one's own dependence on the cultural context to which one belongs. This could lead to a sort of extended, experiential knowledge that is here called *knowing-what-it-is-like*.

Starting with Aristotle's analysis of pity, I shall explore the role of imagination in this specific mode of understanding. I will continue with a discussion of in what sense aesthetic experiences might contribute to the cultivation of moral imagination and compassion, that is, virtues that are of the greatest value for our understanding of others. My aim is also to consider whether we can talk about narrative art as a source for emotional development on an unreflective as well as on a reflective level of being. An emotion is a sign that a person has understood a situation in a certain way. To discuss emotions in terms of understanding is to claim that they are intelligible in a special way. Emotions are, it seems, a kind of value judgment concerning people and situations that are important to ourselves.

We could also talk about emotions in terms of interpretation or "seeing-as." This means that the emotion might evaporate, or perhaps be modified, if we force ourselves to consider another aspect of the situation. Thus, in the second part of this paper, I will discuss how a more reflective and conscious attitude might, when interacting with art, enrich and extend our possibilities for this kind of understanding. Interaction with art may sometimes force us into new ways of looking at ourselves and at our surroundings, a change in attitudes and values that will influence the emotions as well.

Aristotle's Analysis of Pity

Aristotle discusses emotions on several occasions, although in different ways. In the following section, I will analyze his reflections in the *Rhetoric*, and there are many reasons for this. Aristotle still has great influence on the philosophy of emotions, in part because of his way of discussing them in terms of value judgments, and as a way of seeing. He also explicitly emphasizes the importance of discussing emotions through their context, and he chooses his examples from everyday life and poetry.

Aristotle starts his discussion of pity in the *Rhetoric* in the same way he does with all emotions, by offering a definition. He says: "Pity may be defined as a feeling of pain at an apparent evil, destructive or painful, which befalls one who does not deserve it, and which we might expect to befall ourselves or some friend of ours, and moreover to befall us soon."[1] He also reminds us of the connection between fear and pity, and mentions what he calls "the general principle," which is: "what we fear for ourselves excites our pity when it happens to others."[2] An absolute condition for pity, then, is an insight into one's own and one's intimate's frailness and mortality. A consequence of this is that a human being who has nothing to lose, and whose hope and expectations have been dashed, does not have the capability to feel compassion for someone else. Furthermore, cynical and phlegmatic people are incapable of pity, which is also the case with those who are panic-stricken. The reason for the last category is that such people are totally preoccupied with their own problems. Reasons for pity, according to Aristotle, are dreadful things like death, bodily injuries, old age, diseases, etc. But different kinds of evil, like being torn away from friends, or scarcity of friends, can also be the object of pity. The requirement is that we judge the loss, or pain, as being serious. So pity embraces or implies an evaluation, i.e. an evaluation of how significant the situation is for the other person.

Finally, when Aristotle describes for whom we feel pity, we find another interesting observation. Pity, he says, seems generally to embrace people who are close to us. Still, one condition is that they are not too close, because in that case we would feel as if we ourselves were threatened. The question is where this border is actually to be drawn.

Aristotle's example is a man called Amasis, who does not cry when his own son is taken away for execution. In contrast, he did start to weep when he saw a friend begging. Aristotle writes: "The latter sight was pitiful, the former terrible, and the terrible is different from the pitiful; it tends to cast out pity, and often helps to produce the opposite of pity. For we no longer feel pity when the danger is near ourselves."[3] The relationship between the person who pities and the one who is the object of the emotion is thus of importance here. Pity is most easily evoked between friends, colleagues, and neighbors. It seems as if some kind of feeling or concern for the other should already exist, according to Aristotle. What makes pity turn into a painful experience of one's own, i.e. when the balance between thought and feeling evaporates, is when the distance between the person who pities and his object disappears. Closeness in time also seems to be a relevant factor in Aristotle's analysis. Something unpleasant which has just happened, or presumably will occur soon, forces us to feel pity. Things that happened a long time ago, or are supposed to happen in the distant future, do not have the same power. Nonetheless, what is of interest here is the significance of imagination in pity. The emotion can be roused by what *might* happen, whether it in fact happens or not.[4] Both imagination and acting are involved when Aristotle offers another piece of advice to a future orator. He says: "Those who heighten the effect of their words with suitable gestures, tones, appearance, and dramatic action generally, are especially successful in exciting pity: they thus put the disasters before our eyes, and make them seem close to us, just coming or just past."[5]

In Aristotle's analysis we saw that some kind of basic feeling or concern was rather important, although not necessary, for compassion. In the same way, it is interesting to consider the presence of the imaginary in emotions, as imaginary disasters, in Aristotle's opinion, seem to generate pity as well as actual disasters. Initial reflection on this topic gives the impression that imagination perhaps plays a more important role than is usually thought. If emotions are our particular and personal way of understanding a situation, it does seem plausible to claim that what we can imagine about the situation also has relevance for our beliefs regarding that situation.[6] The picture we have of ourselves and of others is of great importance for our understanding of different situations, whether it leads to a specific emotion or not. This picture is part of our self-narratives and is closely connected with what we can possibly imagine about ourselves and the surrounding world.

Knowing-what-it-is-like

If we think that we understand how someone else apprehends his or her situation, we might sometimes take it for granted that we and the other person have a great deal in common like values, expectations, attitudes, etc. Compassion is, among other things, a sharing of values. When a person grieves, her grief embraces her evaluation that she, for instance, has lost something extremely important, like someone she loves. My compassion must understand her grief according to this evaluation. But it is not enough to put oneself in the other person's position; that would miss the whole aspect of the other as a historical, cultural being. One has to consider the qualitative differences between oneself and the other. In order to understand the feelings of a close friend when she has just lost both her parents in an accident, it is not necessary for me to pretend that I have lost both my parents. My friend's whole life story, values, relationship to her parents, etc. are all part of what she is feeling. My relationship to my parents cannot be of much help here.

Let us for a moment look at a discussion about fictional literature in order to explore the mode of understanding I have in mind. Theodore Schick searches for a suitable terminology for the kind of knowledge he thinks we may acquire from fiction. In Schick's opinion, the most valuable knowledge we can get from literature is knowledge about people's experiences. Along with the two kinds of knowledge that are well established, i.e. *knowing-that* and *knowing-how*, Schick mentions a third kind of knowledge—to *know-what*. The difference between knowing-that and knowing-how is easiest to understand by considering the objects of each kind of knowledge. When we talk about knowing-that something, the object of knowledge is a statement or a fact. When it comes to knowing-how something, the knowledge concerns an action. I know that my computer needs electricity in order to work, and I also know how to use it.[7] But what does it mean to know-what? Knowing-what is the kind of knowledge one claims in saying things like: "I know what it is to be poor," "I know what fear is," "I know what it is to be in love," etc. One way, according to Schick, to experience this kind of knowledge is through fictional literature. He says:

> My contention is that experiential knowledge of the knowing-what variety can be communicated through works of fictional literature. Although we do not directly observe or participate in the events presented on the printed page, we sometimes feel as if we directly observe or participate in them. Thus it would appear that sometimes, as a result of reading a work of fictional literature, one is entitled to claim that he knows what it is like to be a certain type of person or to be in a certain type of situation.[8]

The above quotation embraces, in my view, two important keys to how we can relate to things of which we get a description, whether the event actually happened or not. The keys are the words "as if" and "like." If we follow Sartre's thoughts about imagination, we cannot, according to him, perceive and imagine an object at the same time. Roughly speaking, we perceive a present object, and we imagine it when it is absent. If we just turn that assumption the other way round, I presume that the same thing will be the case with our own presence and absence. To feel *as if* you are taking part in a revolution, where masses of people attack the common oppressor, implies an imagination, which is not the case if you feel that *you are* taking part in a revolution. In that case, I would say that you really are taking part in it.

However, to know-what is not always about *as if*. Very often it is a matter of degree. You know to some degree what it is to be hungry if you have spent three days on water and bread. But you know to a much higher degree what it is to be hungry if you have spent three years on water and bread. However, the knowing-what we sometimes get from fiction is not primarily a question of degree. To read about some characters who crash their airplane in the jungle, find an old temple and a lot of gold, are pursued by some strange sect, etc. is not to *know what it is* to be in that situation to some degree; it is to *know what it is like* to be in that situation, perhaps to feel *as if* one were present.

The difference, as it seems, lies between on the one hand remembering something and on the other hand imagining something. Remembering always implies an earlier experience, which is not the case with imagining. Knowing-what-it-is-like is a kind of understanding which is comparable to the kind that is part of compassion. In compassion, you might have your own experience, although it is not necessary. In order to pity someone who has lost her only child, it is not necessary to have had that experience yourself. Compassion is an understanding of the other person's condition and situation, a person who innocently suffers a heavy loss. Parents often force their children into this specific kind of reasoning through utterances like: "How would you feel in his shoes?" or, "Try to imagine what it's like to be in her situation." This reasoning seems to be a kind of skill that we learn in part in childhood. It is practical reasoning, where one has to look at different circumstances of the situation in order to find out how the other person presumably experiences what happens to her. In the imaginary we take the other person's place, considering what we would feel in that situation. The next step is to look at the other's background, experiences, values, etc. in an effort to understand what it is like to be him or her in this situation. It might be misleading to talk about steps, because this is hardly something we do as a reflective analysis. Compassion seems to have this sort of reasoning built into its own structure.

The "Simulation Theory"

But is it appropriate to talk about knowledge when we learn what it is like to be in a fictional character's shoes? In a number of recent articles, Gregory Currie has investigated something that we might call a functionalist aspect of our relationship to fictional narratives. I want to use his reflections here, because they exemplify the kind of practical knowledge I am considering. His suggestion is that we can gain moral knowledge from interaction with fictional narratives. Currie does not claim that this is what is really important about fiction, or that there are no other ways to derive moral knowledge from fiction. His intention instead seems to be to extend the understanding of our engagement in fictional narratives. Essential to Currie's interest are the imaginary and the mental processes which, he thinks, follows from our interaction with fiction. He says: "Imagination might be a source of knowledge; in imagining things, we might thereby come to know (possibly other) things. And if fictions are aids to imagination, they may lead indirectly to knowledge."[9]

In cognitive science, for the last decade or so, there has been a debate going on between theorists who defend the "simulation theory," and those who defend the "theory theory," which are both efforts to explain what we do when we think we know what is going on in another person's mind.[10] The "theory theory," also named "folk psychology," is essentially the idea that in order to understand what another person experiences in a particular situation, we start with some kind of theory, or reasoning, of this person's beliefs and desires. We also have some general principles about how this person will be likely to respond. Given those various premises, we draw our conclusions and claim that we understand what it is for this person to be in this situation.

The "simulation theory" is, in brief, the idea that everybody has an internal simulator. In this simulator we can test-run various strategies, which then function as substitutes for real actions. One purpose of simulation is to try different ways to deal with a situation, but do this, so to say, in safety. Still, the *as if* character of this process will give us an understanding of what it would be like for us to experience it as an actual event. Other things that can be objects of simulation are the mental state of another person and our own contemplated behavior.[11] Currie's work could be seen as a meeting point between aesthetics and cognitive science, and he attempts to find out how "simulation theory" could be applied to aesthetics. According to Currie, imagination is this simulator. Now, "simulation" turns out to be a rather broad concept in Currie's account. Actually, it is equivalent to empathizing, role-playing, and, to some degree, also to remembering. Or, as he says, memory is a "form of simulation."[12]

What we shall look at briefly is the mental process that Currie has in mind. As he claims: "Simulation is defined in terms of the nature of the process itself."[13] Currie describes two orders of imagination, a preliminary and a secondary one. In preliminary imagination, one simulates being someone reading a factual story, and in the secondary imagination, one simulates how one takes on a character's beliefs and desires and makes them one's own in order to understand the character's experience. This is not necessarily a conscious, or even a deliberate action, in Currie's view. Conversely, as fiction functions as an aid to the imaginary, the reader is carried into larger worlds of possibilities than she ever could have hoped to reach by herself. This also means that she can rarely have conscious control all the time.[14] The outcome of this process is that "it will tell us something about how we would respond to the situation, and what it would be like to experience it: a response and a phenomenology we can then transfer to the character."[15]

Following Currie, we find that we have the same kind of practical reasoning in our understanding of fiction that we have in compassion. This is also something he explicitly stresses.[16] The knowledge we acquire is not of a theoretical kind, but of the kind mentioned earlier as knowing-what-it-is-like. This is a process where we learn, not about facts, but to behave in various ways. As Currie claims, interaction with literature may change our lives. Through imaginative involvement with fiction, if things go well, we can obtain moral knowledge and insight that our values are not as we want them to be. This insight can force us to desire other values, and so we begin a chain of events, or a spiral, which in a slow movement leads us to human flourishing.[17]

Moral Imagination

To continuously and consciously look for alternative viewpoints is an obvious foundation for a moral development, according to Mark Johnson. He writes: "No person can be moral in a suitably reflective way who cannot imagine alternative viewpoints as a means of understanding and transforming the limits of his own convictions and commitments. This is an activity of moral imagination."[18] Johnson criticizes the kind of moral reasoning that above all recommends laws and rules for how one ought to act. Rather, the moral identity of an individual is something that takes shape continuously during the whole life, where conceptions, thoughts, and actions are involved in a process dependent on cultural as well as historical conditions.

Both Currie's and Johnson's reasoning confirm the thought that aesthetic experiences might contribute to a person's moral development and identity. Through interaction with other people and art, it is possible to acquire the kind of extended experiential knowledge which is considered here. The sort of practical reasoning that is its foundation is of great value for our relations with other people. This is not simply a question of power and will to imagine how someone else apprehends his or her situation. It is also a question of being able to construct a story and a context that makes the other's emotions and actions understandable. The narrative structure that permeates our lives and is expressed when we talk about our emotions, memories, actions, and dreams, etc. has an obvious connection to fictional narratives. On the one hand, fictions describe situations where emotions and actions occur—situations that furthermore might be beyond our own experience. And on the other hand, our emotional engagement in fictions might in itself lead to understanding. By, for instance, feeling fear in a fictional experience, I claim that it is possible to acquire the kind of understanding which later might force us to feel compassion with other people.

There is a specific connection between pity and fear, as Aristotle shows us when he writes "what we fear for ourselves excites our pity when it happens to others."[19] Stephen Halliwell formulates this intertwining of pity and fear in Aristotle as follows: "So we see confirmed the fine intricacy of this strand of Aristotelian psychology, and its mutually illuminating implications for the experience of tragedy: our pity for others' undeserved suffering depends in part on our sympathetic capacity to imagine, and imaginatively fear, such things for ourselves; and fear for ourselves (though this is not the main element in tragic fear) can in turn be created by the sympathetic experience of others' misfortunes."[20] If emotions evoked by interaction with tragedy in this sense should lead to different modes of insight, it is a question of acknowledging that the characters in many ways are similar to oneself in behavior and possible actions. Through an emotional involvement in their grief, and through a feeling of fear for what might happen, we probably conclude that this situation could also happen to ourselves.

The Inevitable Reflection

In our society, we are often expected to read the other person's mind; this is a somewhat strange expectation, since everyone knows that it is rather impossible. Our efforts nevertheless seem to be valuable in our interaction with others. Still, to imagine how someone else experiences his or her situation is not necessarily of moral value. The method can, for instance, be used by a torturer who wants to find out what would be the most effective implement of torture to use. To turn this into moral imagination, it is essential also to reflect and to go beyond ones own values. Or, in other words, to open one's mind in accordance with what one imagines. Also in this more critical attitude to oneself and the world, fictional narrative might play an important role, which will be the theme of my following discussion. In any event, as I will show, it is not particularly fruitful to try to make a strict distinction between the reflective and the unreflective, as these two levels continuously intermingle and cooperate.

Presumably, it is mostly in discussions with other people that we force ourselves to reflect on aesthetic experiences. In an effort to communicate, we must find new words and formulations. We then participate in the work, shaping a new meaning that reaches beyond the work of art and into our own lives. This participation primarily means discussing art and human life as things that are interconnected and interdependent. An analysis of a fictional character's choice of behavior and action in a specific situation may be useful when we try to reflect on our own or other people's possible decisions as well. Learning how the character moves from anger to love or from jealousy to grief, according to her shifting attitudes and insights, will reveal a wider spectrum of opportunities for ourselves as well. The unreflective mode of understanding, represented by emotions, would probably be very rough and without nuances if we did not reflect on our own and other people's reactions. And here there is one clear connection between language and emotions. If we consider linguistic development and a broad set of concepts as significant for a rich emotional life, we have an obvious link between reading literature and human flourishing. How we articulate and retell a course of events will in the long run have an influence on how we understand a similar situation in the future. Emotions, then, as it seems, are mainly acquired and experienced at a nonreflective level, but are given nuances and refinement reflectively.

The use of a term like "reflection" requires some kind of analysis. The concept has changed historically, and today there is no general agreement on the function and the aims of reflection. What in this context I refer to when discussing reflection is a mode of critical thinking about one's pre-reflective understanding of the world. Reflection, one could say, is to make everything a question. In order to study that question, one describes what is at stake—a description that inevitably will be limited to the vocabulary to which one has access. Reflection in this sense is to make a clarifying description for one's own benefit.[21] Describing his view of reflection, Maurice Merleau-Ponty writes: "Reflection is truly reflection only if it is not carried outside itself, only if it knows itself as reflection-on-an-unreflective-experience, and consequently as a change in structure of our existence."[22] I take Merleau-Ponty's formulation, together with the notion of description, as a fruitful standpoint for the following discussion. To think an event over is to also put words to it, to find the most illuminating and fitting concepts in order to make the situation more graspable. To articulate motives and reactions—one's own as well as others'—is to make an interpretation, where the description also becomes one's personal expression of an understanding.

Articulation and Self-Interpretation

But how do we incorporate what is articulated and reflected in our daily life? In what sense is reflection constitutive of our pre-reflective understanding of ourselves and the world and vice versa? Perhaps we are looking for some kind of movement, a movement between habit and consideration, where one thing shapes the other continuously. Let us take a brief look at Charles Taylor's article "Self-Interpreting Animals" to find support for these ideas.

In his article, Taylor focuses on emotions, and attempts to describe the particular way understanding is represented by emotions and what they tell us about ourselves. By way of introduction, he describes emotions as affective modes of awareness of situations. This involves the claim that an emotion in a sense must be understood as a kind of judgment of the situation in question. But becoming emotional, he continues, means that we do not understand this situation in a neutral or indifferent way. As he argues: "Rather, experiencing an emotion is to be aware of our situation as humiliating, or shameful, or outrageous, or dismaying, or exhilarating, or wonderful; and so on."[23] In short, we are deeply involved ourselves, that is, something matters to us in a serious sense. Taylor prefers to use the term "import," stating that the import in a given situation is what provides, or could provide, the basis for our feelings. Saying what an emotion is like, then, will consequently involve an import-ascription that explicitly refers to our experience and desires. Claiming that a situation is shameful must for this reason mean that we judge the situation in a particular way according to what this concept includes for us, and that there is someone who can experience the emotion in question. Taylor speaks of this as "experience-dependent" and "subject-referring" because an emotion like shame "is about an aspect of the life of the subject *qua* subject."[24] The notion of subject-referring makes it easy to see the difference between two emotions like fear and shame. Shame is closely connected to how one wants to appear in front of other people, in a way that fear is not.

Our sense of dignity, pride, guilt, and related emotions incorporates a sense of what matters to us as human beings in our relationships with others. And this sense, Taylor says, is crucial to our understanding of what it is to be human.

From here it is easy to argue in favor of articulation. That is, some situations can only be understood with regard to certain descriptions. As Taylor writes: "For example, a feeling cannot be one of remorse unless there is a sense of my having done wrong."[25] Certain emotions, he says, involve a certain level of articulation. This is a connection between emotions and language that suits the idea of an emotional development through aesthetic experience. In his discussion of an aesthetic education of emotions, Ronald Hepburn claims that a rich and articulated description of a character's emotions, where the emotion is studied extensively, is emotionally educative. This also includes a nuanced and sensitive description of the situation as such. Thus, further and more refined articulation can in the long run transform and modify our emotional experiences. Reflection and consideration of past events lead to a more complex mode of understanding, which in turn will influence our future experiences of similar situations. As Taylor claims:

> The attempt to articulate is potentially a life-process. At each stage, what we feel is a function of what we have already articulated and evokes the puzzlement and perplexities which further understanding may unravel. ...This is the sense in which man is a self-interpreting animal.[26]

Taylor also makes a distinction between what he calls strong and weak evaluation. Doing this, he explicitly refers to a former distinction between first- and second-order desires.[27] Strong evaluation occurs when our desires themselves become the object of our evaluation. The strong evaluator, then, discriminates between her desires in terms of worth. This, in a sense, is an ethical dimension of emotions as the distinction between immediate desire and merely considered ones, which is rather important for our future plans and life. Thus, how we depict and articulate our future will also have a great impact on our present experience. This might sound like a tough, intellectualized view of ourselves and life. Yet once we are enrolled in language, we can never step outside of it. Our bodies and our pre-reflective understanding of the world are inevitably intertwined with the discourse to which we belong. It should be clear that, like me, Taylor is talking about nuances and differences in kinds of emotions. That is, the emotion might be transformed from one kind of love to another as a result of articulation. If the emotion is transformed into a completely different one, it is because our understanding of the whole situation has altered. The important thing to understand is the circular, or spiral, movement of development, where unreflective experiences cooperate with reflective thinking in an interdependent way.

The Appearance of a Narrative Self

Considering one's emotions, as we have seen, is more than an articulated way of understanding a situation. It is also an interpretation of oneself and one's character. Through expression of emotions, we reveal a great deal about ourselves, not just to other people, but also to ourselves if we take the time to analyze what happens. Reflecting on one's emotions is therefore a source of becoming aware of where one stands evaluatively. It is to recognize one's personal perspective. We could perhaps think of this kind of reflection as a struggle for *knowing-who*. But knowing-who will mostly also imply who-was-I? and who-do-I-want-to-be? The first feature becomes evident in emotions like pride, humiliation, and regret. These emotions are prolonged over time and refer to states of mind that can only be predicated in relation to the past.[28] Conversely, an emotion like love reaches forward, forcing a person to dream, to hope, and to plan for the future.

My relationship to others is the all-embracing context that is of interest here. A self-referring emotion like shame, as already stated, is built on one's relation to the surrounding world. Shame, like other emotions of this kind, includes an awareness of oneself from the point of view of other people. It is interesting that *the other* sometimes might be oneself, in so far as the insight that one is guilty of something blameworthy doubtless could make a person feel ashamed in solitude as well. This makes shame efficacious in the process of socialization. But this self-reference also makes shame, among other emotions, a fundamental feature in our constitution of self. As Anthony Kerby says: "The self, then, comes to itself in and through the other—both the other person that responds to me, and the other that I become in my own self-reflection."[29] Kerby further believes that if Taylor is right in claiming that self-referential emotions arise out of an interpretative framework, then "it should be evident that much of the value of literary works (particularly novels) derives from their articulation and clarification of just why a character undergoes the joys and torments she or he is characterized by."[30]

In his book *Narrative and the Self*, Kerby makes a distinction between the terms "narrative" and "pre-narrative" (or "quasi-narrative"), which may function as a counterpart to our discussion of non-reflective and reflective understanding. According to Kerby, a pre-narrative is an event or action with a genuine narrative structure that has not yet been narrated. He says: "Life is inherently of a narrative structure, a structure that we make explicit when we reflect upon our past and our possible future."[31] An action which has the status of a pre-narrative must be formulated into an explicit narrative understanding in order to lead to any kind of self-understanding. Kerby continues: "To understand ourselves we must grasp our own implicit history, for to be human is not simply to have a history (in a certain sense animals have this), but to be cognizant of this history."[32]

There are thus, according to Kerby, two channels or levels of identity, that is, the level of praxis and the act of self-interpretation. This means that we are engaged in both a receptive and a creative activity in our understanding and narration of ourselves, other people, and the world. This is a never-closing circle or spiral in which a non-reflective and a reflective mode of being cooperate, with both levels equally important to a person's development and sense of self. New forms of articulation, new ways of looking at things, metaphors, distinctions, and different kinds of linguistic experiments will make narratives an inevitable asset on this account as well.[33]

Notes

1.   Aristotle, *Rhetoric*, 1385b, 13-16. I will in the following discussion use "pity" and "compassion" as interchangeable. Cf. Nussbaum, 1996, p. 29.
2.   Aristotle, *Rhetoric*, 1386a, 28.
3.   Aristotle *Rhetoric*, 1386a, 21-25.
4.   For a discussion of this aspect, see Nehamas, 1994, p 269.
5.   Aristotle, *Rhetoric*, 1386a, 31-34.
6.   In a lecture on emotions and rationality in Stockholm, October 1998, Martha Nussbaum stated that we can have the right beliefs about what is happening in a situation, but the wrong beliefs about the value, or importance, of what is happening.
7.   Gilbert Ryle formulates the differences between these two kinds of knowledge. Ryle, 1952, pp. 25-62.
8.   Schick, 1982, p. 37.

9. Currie, 1998, p. 161.
10. The two different standpoints are discussed in e.g.: Davies and Stone (eds.), 1995a and Davies and Stone (eds.), 1995b, as well as Carruthers & Smith (eds.), 1996 and in several volumes of *Mind & Language*.
11. Currie, 1995a, p. 158.
12. Currie, 1997, p. 74.
13. Currie, 1996, p. 245.
14. Currie, 1995a, p. 163.
15. Currie, 1995b, p. 257. I am not sure that I agree with Currie here. There is a freedom in our relationship with art that we do not have when we claim that we understand another person's mental state. In interaction with art, it is enough to consider what we ourselves would feel in the situation described. We do not have to transfer it to the character in order to gain moral knowledge. Robert Sharpe suggests that a kind of "reverse simulation" is more common than the one ordinarily discussed. He writes: "I learn about myself by looking at others. I see somebody envious of his neighbor's new car and think to myself 'Do I act like that?' The thought is sobering. Certainly the moral effect of literature may often be of this form" (Sharpe 1997:126).
16. Currie, 1997, p. 70.
17. For a somewhat similar account, cf. Anthony Savile in his discussion of Aristotle and Schiller and their statements of the importance of art regarding our understanding of the world. Savile, 1982, pp. 86-108.
18. Johnson, 1993 p. 203.
19. Aristotle, *Rhetoric*, 1386a, 27.
20. Halliwell, 1986, p. 177. According to Halliwell though, the association of pity and fear was not original with Aristotle, but can be traced back to Homeric epic, Sophocles, Gorgias, and Plato. Cf., Ibid., 170.
21. Cf. Faber, 1947-48, pp. 588-600.
22. Merleau-Ponty, 1995, p. 62. The quotation is from Donald Verene's exposé on different philosophers' application of "reflection," starting with Descartes, who coins the concept in his *Discourse of Method* 1631. Verene, 1997, chap. 1.
23. Taylor, 1985, p. 48.
24. Taylor, 1985, p. 55.
25. Taylor, 1985, p. 63.
26. Taylor, 1985, p. 65.
27. Frankfurt, 1971, pp. 5-20. For criticism of Taylor's notion of strong evaluation, see for instance: Flanagan, 1990, pp. 37-65, and Slote, 1988, pp. 379-387.
28. Cf. Freeman, 1993, p. 93.
29. Kerby, 1986, p. 217.
30. Kerby, 1986, p. 217.
31. Kerby, 1991, p. 40. Kerby explicitly makes references to Paul Ricoeur throughout his discussion, and in his article "Life: A Story in Search of a Narrator," Ricoeur works with an argumentation analogous to Kerby's. See Ricoeur, 1991, pp. 425-437.
32. Kerby, 1991, p. 87.
33. See also Elam, 2001.

4

Autonomy's Sources and the Impact of Globalization

John Dunn

I

Europeans, to use an anachronistic but still pertinent category, have been quarreling about the sources, grounds, and consequences of the virtues for some time. In the lengthy perspective of these quarrels, the judgment that autonomy is and must be the pivot or core of the virtues is a relatively recent innovation—roughly coeval with the epoch labeled by Alasdair MacIntyre as lying *After Virtue*.[1] It is a European eccentricity, and perhaps a rather eccentric European eccentricity at that. But its source, insofar as it lies within this world at all, lies not in Europe itself, but in the ancient, tortured, blood-drenched landscape of Palestine.

If it is to be exhibited anywhere, and on however extensive a human stage, it must first be present, and rather robustly present, within at least one individual human being. Given its historical recency and geographical idiosyncrasy, everything hangs on quite how it gets there. As Michel Foucault demonstrated so indefatigably, this is the sort of question about which it is exceedingly easy to confuse oneself, and quite hard (perhaps all but impossible), however clear-headed, learned, and honest you contrive to become, to escape some measure of confusion.[2] Once autonomy comes to be valued highly, it will, like any other highly valued characteristic, be widely aped. Ersatz autonomy, the more or less proficient simulation of autonomy, may well be overwhelmingly commoner than the real thing. Hypocrisy, we are assured, is the homage that vice pays to virtue; and for many it is likely to prove a considerably cheaper form of homage than the service of virtue itself. If we are to fathom where autonomy comes from, we must first look as hard as we dare for the boundary lines between ersatz and genuine autonomy, or, if the idea of bright-line divisions between the two proves implausible in the face of psychological or sociological exploration, we must sharpen any prior suspicions we might have had over the clarity and authority of the concept in the first place. If we choose to pursue our inquiries through the methods of social science, by studying human behavior in an iterative and presumptively reliable manner, we must interrogate that behavior sternly to distinguish the ersatz from the authentic: true autonomy from its poised and fluent impostors.

Autonomy has an elusive conceptual standing in the first instance. It is both a categorical presupposition for genuine virtue within the most influential modern deontological theory, and a notably exacting virtue in itself (or at any rate a formidable personal power that may well seem a virtue when exercised in a style, and for apparent purposes, which the appraiser in question happens to approve). In this sense it is far more deeply at odds with consequentialism than with either deontology or what has come to be known as Virtue Ethics—the view that moral evaluation should center instead on concrete human psychological dispositions, powers, and character traits.[3] As a disposition, power, or character trait, autonomy demands a certain obduracy: an imperviousness to the threats and blandishments of other human beings. But as a virtue or precondition for virtue, it plainly requires something else as well: not merely a deafness to the more or less well-meaning harassments of others, but also a deliberate subjection of the self to a range of principles or values which fully deserve respect or even devotion in their own right.

The power to resist external human pressure at the point of action must be complemented by, and placed in the service of, an eager responsiveness to the right set of external moral, political, and perhaps even spiritual coordinates. This is an inherently unstable balance. In the course of the last three centuries it has become clear that it can tip over in a great many different and sometimes dismaying directions. Who is to say what *does* deserve such respect or devotion, and just when are they to say it? Who is to define the right set of coordinates, and when exactly in relation to the human life cycle (birth, childhood, adolescence, maturity, in the face of death)[4] are they to do so? Just how are they to do so? In what voice, through what channels, and by what authority? What answers, if any, to these questions can hope to hold up in face of autonomy's endless challenge? Show me why I should. Show me that I should. Show me that for *me* in particular, as I am and feel and see at this very moment, that you really are right to judge that *I should*. Make your intrusive and condescending judgment my own, and do so in my full view, and in the teeth of at least some elements of my sentiments and perceptions at the time. (Of course, if it happens to coincide with these sentiments and perceptions, you need not bother—your efforts will be otiose. But that is because autonomy under those circumstances is wholly irrelevant, just beside the point.) Where autonomy matters is where the way in which it is exercised or displayed is itself under suspicion. And when it is, how are we to tell that autonomy is indeed a virtue, and not a peculiarly offensive form of vice—an independently ascertainable vice, with the added odium of self-righteousness?

Foucault is the modern thinker who has thought most intriguingly about these questions.[5] What makes his thought so stimulating is its unflinching focus on the ineradicable ambivalence of autonomy, its delicate blend of courage and arrogance, and on the queasy psychic and social sources of all the powers and pretensions of human agency at its least limp, passive, heteronymous, or subjugated. He saw the enforcement of predictability, cooperation, and conformity in society as both a source of new human powers and an instance of repression. The elevation of autonomy as coping stone to all the virtues glories in its contribution to extending human powers, but has the greatest difficulty in reconciling this posture with due acknowledgement of the scale and intricacy of repression needed to sustain it. Everyone who becomes autonomous to any degree does so by courtesy of a great deal else—of much which is unmistakably prior in time and external in space to their own self-legislated and fully self-secured agency.[6] How should we see these external sources of this very general power or accomplishment: what it is outside the person that places the power or accomplishment in the end fully within their grasp?

Behind the concerns of this volume lies the fear, or at the very least the acute anxiety, not so much that our core continuing social practices in North America, Britain, or above all Sweden itself, may not make entirely coherent sense, as that the relatively clear and more or less urgently cherished sense which they did or still do make faces rising threats from economic, social, political, or even cultural and intellectual processes which we have little, if any, power to restrain. There is good reason to suppose that Foucault was right to assume that many of these practices never did make entirely clear sense and that there is little prospect of their ever coming to do so in future. But there is also good reason to suppose, with Burke but perhaps again with Foucault too, that we have been on balance quite right to cherish them, and that we would prove in retrospect to have altogether better reason to mourn than to applaud their passing. Potential threats to the more cherished social virtues (trustworthiness, generosity, civility, patience, kindness, and so on) might come from many quarters. Some have seen the main source of threats in the extension in the scale and intensity of human interaction itself—in what is blearily called globalization, in the ever-more blatant de-insulation, practical and imaginative, of all the settings in which human beings live, work, and divert themselves.

There is little reason to endorse this presumption. But it is hard to exaggerate how pervasive this motif has become over the last four centuries of European thinking. I doubt greatly myself whether spatial scale, or even celerity of communication, have anything to do with the matter. But it is important to pin down where the appeal of this imagery comes from. In the end, probably, it comes from a quite accurate recognition that the more or less fluent exercise of any apprehensible range of the virtues will always be a strenuous and precarious achievement for any human society, and from the attempt to frame the challenge of reaching this standard on the model of well-considered and prospectively effective collective action. The more strenuous the achievement, surely, the greater the need to act together, and do so fluently and vigorously, to pull it off; the more unnerving the prospect of fellow members actively subverting the presumed aims; and the more obvious the need for a stage that can be seen clearly, at least in the mind's eye (cf. Lantz above), and across which the architects of virtue can hope to reach as far, as potently, and as dexterously as they will certainly need to.

Block any of these conditions, and the very idea of generating and sustaining even the more indispensable of social virtues by acting together becomes simply quixotic: a conservative social romanticism, dissipated forever by the relentless march of History, or Capital, or Disenchantment. The communitarians complain that liberalism rots society itself, dissolving disciplined and public-regarding effort of the right kind into the smug whimsicalities of myriads of individual "life plans," and probably into quite a lot of the unmistakable vice which naturally issues from such plans when they come to be implemented in practice. Liberals respond that communitarians show themselves wholly obtuse to, and implicitly reject, the demands of autonomy—the master virtue—or perhaps even the key precondition for any virtue at all. This is not an edifying quarrel, and it carries little guaranteed instruction. But what it perhaps does do is to bring out the scale on which disbelief must be suspended in any human society for it to see itself as reliably capable, through its own well-understood operations, of generating the human performance capabilities required for its own flourishing. To insist that these capabilities be manifested, individual by individual, and in each instance, by his or her own free choice (autonomously) drastically heightens the requirements for belief—raising them to an all but hysterical pitch. And it notably fails to indicate how they could be met in principle, let alone why in practice they are likely to be met at all.

To see autonomy as the key personal virtue, to see it, as Dworkin does,[7] as indissolubly linked to the sovereign social virtue of equality, is to look at collective social life in a generous but singularly optimistic way, to think of it as though it might ideally consist in a vast range of complementary fulfillments and rewards, and not in an inherently painful, confused, and unprepossessing trade-off between an equally vast range of interpersonal and impersonal bads. There is something to be said for thinking of ethics—the theory of the good individual human life—either way round, and perhaps more in the very last instance in this case for the former than for the latter. What, in the end, is the point of life after all, but to *live* it as well as one can?[8] And how can there be a more continuously urgent question for any of us than just how well that is? In face of that question, too obsessive a consequentialism can simply make you lose your grip on the issue—to forget quite what it was you were trying to understand. But there is considerably less to be said for thinking of politics in the same way. Politics is concerned not with transcending the conflicts within individuals, but with handling for the better the conflicts between them.[9] It can have other and nobler preoccupations and objectives; but it can never afford to allow its attention to stray too far from its central and inescapable task. To see what that task is and assess how best to discharge it demands a very large measure of consequentialism. It requires that we look at human agents and human actions, not tenderly and yearningly from the inside, but firmly from the outside, and with quite a high level of suspicion.

A simple political perspective on the normative standing of autonomy splits it in the first instance by focusing on the manner of its exercise, and assessing this, quite unapologetically, principally in terms of its apparent net consequences over time for others than the agent in question. It values highly exercises of autonomy which it judges consequentially benign, and attaches little, if any, determinate value to autonomy exerted with seriously malign consequences. It is less interested in the degree to which it is phenomenologically, ontologically, psychologically, or sociologically realistic to see the agents in question as full causes of their own actions than in the implications of those actions for other human beings then or later. It is therefore overwhelmingly more at ease, in Berlin's classic, if rough and ready, contrast, with negative rather than positive conceptions of liberty.[10] It takes the task of furnishing mutual security and protection altogether more urgently than that of nurturing the sense of integrity and self-actualization within individual lives. You might conclude from this that thinking too much about politics disables one from recognizing or taking in the main elements of the human good, or that it shows something of peremptory importance about the human good that cannot be clearly apprehended from within the workings of the personal sensibility of individuals alone. If you have stout nerves and a good deal of patience, you might even conclude both.[11]

Whatever you conclude, a political perspective on autonomy must stick with the contrast between consequentially benign and consequentially malign autonomy; reject the claim that the latter is a virtue; reject the judgment that the unassessed capacity for choice deserves to be valued in itself (at least wherever it certainly will be exercised with actively malign consequences); and insist instead that the care of society, which is a necessary counterpart to Foucault's explorations of the history of care for the self,[12] requires a steady and un-self-deceptive grasp of just what needs to be true of human beings for them to be likely to *choose* at all consistently to act not merely for their own benefit, but to the net advantage of their fellows.

It is not clear that this is a field in which the modern social sciences have made any reliable headway. Partly because of this rather obtrusive failure (so drastically at odds with the expectations of many of the luminaries of the Enlightenment) in the formally democratic states and economically insecure societies of Europe today, none of us at present, in any of our roles, from the most private to the most public, can reasonably be confident that we do understand how to form or sustain the social virtues on which we continue to depend for so much of our own flourishing. One important reason why this might be so is a certain unevenness in dispersed cognitive advance as opposed to dexterous human molding—a mismatch between cumulative and increasingly heterogeneous skepticism, and the ingenuity, the imaginative courage, and the normative composure with which we envisage socialization. For academic analysts this raises a painful question. Is this mismatch an inevitable consequence of the uncontrollable impetus of cognitive advance, or is it simply a product of misallocation of attention, or aberration within what Adam Smith called "the moral sentiments?"[13] Are we just the messengers bringing the more or less dismaying news that was always objectively there—in the genetic makeup of our species, and the ineluctable dynamics of its dispersion across the world over time?[14] Or is the outcome a collective indiscretion of the modern intelligentsia, a consequence of one, or a great many, wrong turnings, taken relatively recently, or very long ago? It would be nice to know. But what is clear, even without knowing, is that the latter possibility is not one which anyone who elevates autonomy into the master virtue or key to all the virtues can decently shrug off. At the very least they should take the trouble to work out a compelling reason to believe the opposite.

II

Globalization, like every large-scale political or economic process, is an extravagantly complex blend of choice and fate. Even as choice, moreover, it is plainly also something other and more than an indiscretion of the Western intelligentsia, who have been divided sharply throughout in their attitudes towards it. Yet it remains a question of the keenest interest how far globalization has in practice enhanced the autonomy of different groups of human beings, and how far such gains in autonomy as it has delivered have been applied in practice for the advantage or disadvantage of other human beings.

The three main dimensions of globalization are given by shifts in the speed, scale, and depth or intensity, of human interaction.[15] For anyone whose sense of human potentiality leads them to view their fellows, individually or by composition, with some degree of apprehension, all three shifts might well sharpen that apprehension, principally because they up the ante, augmenting the scale of possible consequences, for the worse as for the better, and extending the range of circumstances with which we must try to reckon. They multiply the candidates for worst case scenarios, and underline disconcertingly the virtual certainty that the world in which anyone who is now alive, and will still be living half a century later, will be bewilderingly different in ways most of us cannot hope to begin to anticipate.

You might think that the correct appraisal of the overall significance of globalization must be that it multiplies the given human potential for better or worse across the board, by a single large (if never, to us, wholly determinate) value, making the best far better and the worst far worse, and changing everything in between more or less in proportion. Or, if you have a more archaic sensibility, or a gloomier disposition, you might think that it vastly increases the potentiality for harm but does nothing to enhance the best that humans can hope for—since that best can never be more than a minimal spiritual edification of an unenticing animality: a measure of self-control, a modicum of mutual consideration, a grudging and somewhat myopic quotient of practical altruism, which has to be secured, if it is to be secured anywhere, at the level of the individual soul.

Neither of these views is simply imbecilic, and it is far from clear that neither is simply right. But what is clear is that neither constitutes a serious attempt to answer the key question social scientists, between them, should at least be professionally equipped to answer as cogently as any humans can. That question is not about the best or worst that could happen because of globalization, as the latter continues on its way. It is about what is likeliest to happen: what outcomes are most probable as the species moves forward in its headlong flight through space and time? The sole resource we possess for thinking about that question is thinly specified hypotheticals: a weak instrument at the best of times, and especially treacherous when culture, temperament, and even political animus leak so permanently and comprehensively into the hypotheses we even choose to consider.[16] We choose these hypotheses because they seem to *us* appropriate, plausible, or illuminating, or worse still because we expect them to favor political conclusions we already strongly support, or entrepreneurial ventures in which we have already invested heavily.

And then we try to persuade one another of the felicity of these hypothetical formats for grasping how the human future is likely to turn out, and how we should see it and feel about it. In this exercise much is sometimes at stake practically, and almost everything human is potentially at issue epistemologically. But there is one large strategic issue of judgment that is always at stake: the epistemological terms of trade between normative assessment and causal betting. The entire history of Western political and social thought is an imaginative struggle for hegemony over this great issue: in a less explicit, but perhaps equally solid sense, perhaps the whole history of human politics.[17] If we interrogate the future in essentially normative terms, following however clumsily in the footsteps of Kant, it is hard to avoid envisaging it in ways that virtually eliminate causality—which see it as a space where, wherever politics or social and economic reality now are, ethical theory should be instead. If we ignore normativity altogether—simply suspend our normative attention until we have finished placing our bets—the perspective becomes so unfamiliar that it is hard to make up our minds at all. The net causal weight of normative awareness is anyone's guess. (Do you think you know how to judge it? And if you do, how do you think you came by that knowledge?)

In the history of modern political, economic, and social thought—a Western invention under erratic and severely incomplete transformation into a global apparatus of orientation and analysis—the key category for organizing these hypotheticals has been the division of labor, privileged site of technical change, the structuring and organization of authority, and the putatively rational contours of group identification.[18] Through its interpretation, for several hundred years, a vast range of thinkers and political or economic actors have sought to interpret which formats or units of action their audiences or human targets had good reason to confide in, and which formats or units they had even better reason to distrust or loathe. In assessing the degree of ambivalence which we owe to globalization, one natural way to try to make up our minds is to ask how far it moves power and choice away from sites and agencies we have good reason to trust to others that are far less trustworthy, and how far it does precisely the opposite. Here the prevalent suspicion recently has been that globalization does indeed move power and choice quite brusquely away from the privileged aspirants to effective representation over most of modern politics—from nation states, for example, prospectively loyal at least to the interests of their own nationals, or well set up to adjudicate coherently and act effectively on behalf of a common national interest, or from political parties, potentially equipped to take over those state powers and direct them fluently, at least for a time, to serve the interests of the classes, regions, or religious groupings they undertake to represent. More dubiously but encouragingly, also, over the last decade and a half, many have seen a pronounced shift from pathological to benign forms of state (from autocracy to representative democracy),[19] or from ingenuously malignant political parties, domestic economic policies, and international trade regimes to distinctly sounder alternatives (from socialism, inflationary demand management, and manipulated foreign trade, to a wall-to-wall amalgam of global liberalism and domestic fiscal prudence). More vaguely still, others have seen the key political significance of globalization as lying not in what it does to or within or through states, but in the degree to which it enhances the relative power or future prospects of quite different sorts of organization or agency: Global Democracy or economic governance, a myriad of NGOs, a virtually extraterritorial phalanx of transnational economic corporations. If you think that some of these are, ex ante, clearly more trustworthy and others clearly less so, and if you think that globalization definitely enhances the scope and power of some and diminishes the scope and power of others, then those thoughts alone are enough to imply that globalization is indeed already making (and will probably, unless God in His mercy or malignity intervenes, continue to make) the human world safer or more perilous, kinder and gentler, or even uglier, than it previously used to be. What is important to see about this judgment is that its weight falls not on a view of globalization itself, but on a multiplicity of views about categories, or forms of institution, of which Western thinkers have been thinking for some time, and which they have by now, between them, made considerable progress in understanding.

Is globalization, then, a friend or an enemy, a ground for hope or for despair, a stunning achievement or an ever-more overwhelming predicament? There is nothing wrong with these questions. They may be crassly expressed; and they sound unsophisticated. But they must have answers; and the answers must matter enormously for us. What may require some apology, however, is that the right answers are bound to prove fairly disappointing. To think effectively about globalization and its human impact, one needs to break it up carefully into a huge range of opaquely interacting practices, as David Held and his colleagues, for example, have recently done,[20] and then think very carefully about the properties of each of the practices distinguished, and how these do in fact interact, and to judge how much plasticity there really is in their potential interaction in the future. In short, one needs to think *politically*, and do so in as attentive, vigilant, un-self-deceived, and energetic a manner as possible. If this is done with minimal competence, one will certainly conclude that globalization is all of these things. It is a friend and an enemy, a ground for hope and a ground for despair (or at least for the most acute anxiety), a stunning achievement and an ever-more overwhelming predicament. It cannot yet be known whether what is going on today is that we are already hurtling towards a common disaster that we have no chance whatever of avoiding (the interactive political analogue of a huge asteroid strike), or instead at last beginning to establish, however erratically, an ever-steadier control over the practical challenges of collective human life. Globalization is an inordinately vague description of any features of the human world, and scarcely even the rudiment of an instrument for analyzing whatever features it does contrive to describe. But it is a serviceable initial name for some of the features that hold the most promise, and for some of those which hold the most menace, for the human future.

It pulls together in a single word the widest scale and most elaborate of the practices of collaboration that human beings have thus far developed, and the most extravagant edifices of mutual threat and the most blatantly reckless modes of material gratification we have yet devised. Military globalization, ecological globalization, communicative globalization, all of these create huge opportunities for collective betterment—pacification, recapturing control over the awesome negative externalities of modern economic activity, mutual access, the staggering increase in our collective capacity to reshape the practical components of our lives. But they also, all too obviously, create quite unprecedented opportunities for damaging human life chances now and in the future, on a scale that has no clear cutoff point short of the extinction of our species and whatever else it takes with it.

Short of this terminal disaster, we nevertheless cannot know how it is going to come out, as at that time there will be none of us left to tell. All we can judge reasonably accurately is which aspects of these myriad and infinitely differentiated processes are for the moment improving human opportunities or enhancing human life styles, and which very definitely are not. To think politically about how we should assess globalization, we must (and all, of course, in fact will) bring to bear the ways in which we habitually seek to grasp politics, in all their variety and widely varying felicity. To judge the political significance of globalization for the present, the harm and good it has done already, and the accessible room for future damage and improvement it is now opening up, it is instructive to start by asking why it has come out as badly as it now has. One can look at human life chances, the organization of economic activity, and the articulation of power across the globe, and ask how far and how tightly they fit together, and how deeply embedded the vast burden of individual suffering and degradation really is in the economic, political, and social structuring of a single interconnected field of power and organization.

Insofar as we can learn how to do this, we can hope to answer the question of why the human world is still as grim as it unmistakably is for vast numbers of our fellows. Even if it *is* true that the average human being now lives in more eligible circumstances, and perhaps on balance on more acceptable terms than his counterpart did even a hundred years ago, it is also all too probable that more human beings now live in more appalling circumstances and on terms that are more utterly abominable than at any of humanity's earlier stages. (The scale of the increase in human population in the poorer countries over the last three-quarters of a century has virtually guaranteed that this must be so.) This is not an encouraging thought and gives some occasion for historical shame. It would be good to be at least reasonably certain that this will not still be true in a century's time. If we really understood *why* the human world is still as grim as it is, there would be little danger (given both our inalienable freedom and our buoyant ingenuity) that we would discover that it simply *has* to be that grim. What is not obvious (and perhaps has not been seriously illuminated by more than a century of professionalization of the social sciences) is whether or not we would discover that it is far likelier than not to remain that grim as far as the eye can see.

To judge this seriously, we still need to get a grip on a number of archaic issues. Where does the capacity and propensity to behave well come from in human beings? What are the fundamental psychodynamics of ethical susceptibility and character formation? In the end, over the politics of globalization, these are not soft issues of rhetoric or euphemism (to be left to pious preliminary mumblings or vapid concluding perorations). Instead, they are hard issues of ultimate political explanation. If generosity and decency and self-control and courage come *from* somewhere in particular, we need to know what it is that they do come from, what makes them possible, what makes them even likely, what makes them all but certain. We need to know how far we can foster them deliberately in our own families or universities or political parties, our public bureaucracies and great business enterprises, our favored NGOs, even, dare I say it, our own selves. We need to know how far they remain (and for all that we can yet tell may always remain) at the mercy of genetics and interactive good and ill fortune. We need to know how deeply ecologically unfavorable the structures of our collective life today really are to their survival or regular exercise, and how far these structures can be made less inimical to them and more hearteningly supportive of them. This is more an endless political fight and an open intellectual agenda than a closed structure of fatality, or a comfortingly providential and pre-established habitat.

This is why personal trust and distrust is still such a highly cathected theme in contemporary politics.[21] We need to trust what we know to be far from trustworthy. We need to shoulder risks that we know to be excessive. We need to suspend our disbelief in a controlled, alert, but disturbingly self-exposing way. If we hold our disbelief proudly intact, press our interests coolly and deftly against all comers, never permit ourselves to be shown up as suckers, the globe that we will leave behind us will be unimaginably hideous, and the lives of our descendants as odious as the courts of Nero or Caligula. But why should we believe that this is the way that it is bound to turn out? Ingenuousness and cynicism have fought each other the whole way through human history. Why should either, all of a sudden, register a clean win? (Indeed, how could either?)

III

Ethical susceptibility, openness to shame and guilt, recognition of the harm we are doing and the good we clearly are not but so easily might, and the virtues that can only be built out of these materials, all of these depend on some level of intimacy with other human beings—on our imaginative co-presence with them, our apprehension that they too are fully there, and of what their being so means for them.[22] Globalization does not enforce imaginative intimacy on anyone. It neither disrupts the more formidable psychic barriers to its creation, nor reaches past the very extensive informational obstacles in its way. Most of us have some difficulty in reaching much intimacy with anyone else at all (not infrequently, even with our selves). We can confidently expect this to continue to be so of our descendants. But what globalization certainly does do is to make it possible to communicate with our fellows on a scale never before even imaginable, and in an endlessly proliferating variety of ways. It is an external and structural facility for supporting and instructing ethical susceptibility, however much of an affront to that susceptibility much of its causal architecture now offers and is all but certain to continue to provide. But the ethical susceptibility itself, and its more or less clumsy transposition into political action, those are still unremittingly up to us.

Like globalization itself, autonomy neither guarantees nor precludes intimacy. It neither guarantees nor precludes sympathy. It neither guarantees nor precludes self-sacrifice. If we think of autonomy as a metric for social achievement, and ask how far different societies today contrive to maximize it, we can be confident of some of the answers: Holland and Florida, plainly, more than Liberia or Afghanistan. This paints the globe neatly in one set of ideological colors. But if we ask how far globalization promotes or impedes the maximization of autonomy in different settings, we should expect a somewhat different cartographic pigmentation. Some aspects of the distribution of autonomy will certainly appear (and others will in fact be) clearly zero-sum in character. The autonomy of some will be all too evidently a reciprocal of the heteronomy of others. Dworkin is right to insist that there is something deeply egalitarian about elevating autonomy to the master virtue.[23] But globalization is a profoundly inegalitarian process: a pure game of power. The fit today between our ethical and our political intuitions could hardly be more precarious. And all this, even before we make the slightest attempt to take economic causality into account. Autonomy may well offer the best candidate for a normative metric. (The view that it does has a lengthy and imposing philosophical ancestry in a number of different cultures.) What is very clear is that as of yet we have only the haziest conception of how to apply that metric coherently in practice to the world in which we now live. Whatever else it may signify, this is a cataclysmic failure in political intelligence.

Notes

1. MacIntyre, 1981.
2. Foucault, 2001.
3. Geuss, 2000, p. 6.
4. Bostock, 2001 and Tolstoy, 1960.
5. Foucault, 1981-90 and 2001.
6. MacIntyre, 1999.
7. Dworkin, 2000.
8. Dworkin, 2000.
9. Dunn, 2000.
10. Berlin, 1969.
11. Cf. Dunn, 2000, Geuss, 1980 and 2001.
12. Foucault, 1990.
13. Smith, 1976.
14. Dunn, 2000.
15. Held et al., 1999.
16. Dunn, 2000.
17. Cf. Dunn, 1996.
18. Dunn, 1980, Dunn (ed.), 1990, "Conclusion," Przeworski, 1985.
19. Fukuyama, 1992, cf. Dunn (ed.), 1992.
20. Held et al., 1999.
21. Dunn, 1990 and 2000.
22. Dunn, 1990 and 2000.
23. Dworkin, 2000.

5

Personal Independence and Social Justice: Contradictions of Liberal Virtues?

Ludvig Beckman

The prominent element in Justice as ordinarily conceived is a kind of Equality: that is, Impartiality.... But when we have clearly distinguished this element, we see that the definition of the virtue required for practical guidance is left obviously incomplete.—*Henry Sidgwick,* The Method of Ethics, *1906, p. 269.*

It is common to explain the presence or lack of social justice in terms of the performance of institutions. Social injustice is considered to be a consequence of the way political and economic institutions work rather than a consequence of the way individuals act. Thus, in order to rectify unjust societies there tends to be a call for new institutions rather than a new people.

Although there are certainly good reasons to emphasize the importance of institutions, this view may encourage the perception that political standards of justice do not apply to individuals at all. The recent fate of the former minister for justice of the Swedish government, Laila Freivalds, is a good illustration of this. The Social Democratic government, of which she was a member, had long opposed and attempted to prevent local authorities from selling public property to individuals. Freivalds' Department of Justice was in fact preparing legal changes that would circumvent these developments. However, when Freivalds' family was given an offer to purchase public property, she accepted it. The media and the public immediately reacted, and Freivalds had to leave the government in September 2000.

To some extent this affair illustrates the power of the media, but it also illustrates the power of personal standards of justice. Apparently, the charge leveled against Freivalds concerned her failure to consider justice as relevant to personal and not only to political conduct. As it seemed, leading members of the government did not believe that political principles of justice should translate into standards for personal conduct.[1]

Arguably, this low estimation of personal virtues of justice is prominent in political thinking as well as in political practice. The dominant ideology of our Western culture, Liberalism, establishes standards of social justice that direct political action as well as political criticism. Governments are criticized whenever they seem to pursue discriminatory policies or when they fail to address increasing poverty. Yet, it seems that it does not include standards for assessing the justness of personal conduct.

Recently, Gerald Cohen turned against this tendency in our political thinking.[2] Cohen argues that dominant political theories are too occupied with the importance of just institutions, and too little concerned with the importance of just people. The claim is that people who believe in the need for redistributive justice could do a lot more to promote just distributions than they do. But liberals are likely to hesitate before this view. Cohen argues that the reason for this is the common assumption of these theories "that the demands placed by justice on government do not belong on the back of the individuals."[3]

In what follows, I will accept the relevance of Cohen's critique. The importance of the virtues of justice is, I believe, unduly neglected in contemporary liberal thinking. However, I also believe that Cohen is not adequately taking into consideration the ambiguous liberal attitude to virtues. I will argue that distinguishing between political and ethical liberalism has consequences for the issue raised by Cohen.[4] The aim of this essay is, in other words, to push Cohen's charges a little further and to describe the new dilemma faced by ethical liberals: accommodating the virtues of justice and the virtues of independence.

The Question

The question asked by Cohen concerns the relevance of personal conduct to theories of social justice. However, the charge is not that liberals ignore personal conduct completely. Indeed, such a claim would be absurd. Surely, liberals would accuse anyone of hypocrisy who did not accept the cost of his or her convictions. If, for example, you believe in the need for redistributive policies, you have to eat your words unless you happily accept the taxes that make possible child allowances, welfare checks, age pensions, and other benefits. Thus, what is at stake here is not the discrepancy between conviction and action, which is common enough. We are concerned with a discrepancy between different convictions: between standards of institutional justice and standards of personal justice.

The distinction is seen once the previous example is modified a little. Assuming that you find public welfare in your society to be far from adequate and that you have a certain degree of faith in the efficiency of state bureaucracy, you would be happy to pay more taxes than you presently do. Yet is this all you need to do, in order to avoid having to eat your own words? In fact, this case is somewhat different from the former. Here you are asked to happily accept a *hypothetical* burden (the taxes you *should* pay) whereas in the former case you were asked to happily accept an *existing* burden (the taxes you *do* pay). But is accepting a hypothetical burden really to accept a burden at all? In fact, as long as taxes are lower than you think they should be, the costs of your convictions is zero. Talk is cheap, as they say.

In order for the latter case to be parallel to the former, we consequently need to introduce some real burdens. This could be achieved by assuming, for example, that you freely give some portion of your income away as long as taxes have not been raised to the level supposed to be just. Thus, if you believe taxes are too low you will happily accept increased taxation, but also happily accept giving some of your personal wealth away in the meantime. The crucial question now is: Would liberals ask you to do that? I do not think so. Liberal criticism of individuals not being just enough seems rather infrequent.

Political Liberalism

The charge that the virtues of justice are unduly neglected is especially relevant to "political liberalism." A defining feature of this doctrine is that the focus of justice is restricted to the "the basic structure of society."[5] The basic structure includes society's main political, economic, and social institutions. In order to realize social justice, these institutions need to be ordered according to the principles of justice.

There has been some argument about what exactly the notion of "the basic structure" refers to. The ambiguity of the concept is reflected in the uncertainty of whether the basic structure refers to society's most coercive institutions, or if it refers to the institutions that are causally most important.[6] However, essential for the sake of the present discussion is whether the basic structure includes people's virtues or not. In case it does not, the conclusion will be that a just society could be established without the citizenry necessarily being virtuous at all. Taking literally the claim that justice only requires the formal institutions of society to be just, the conclusion would be that social justice is compatible with an intentionally vicious citizenry.

The comforts of a political system where everything depends on the performance of institutions, and nothing on the performance of individuals, would naturally be great. A socially just world without morally just people makes an attractive picture, since it seems to spare us much trouble. As has been noted, the blessings of institutional justice allow us "to achieve our egalitarian aims without making ourselves miserable in the process."[7] Ardent egalitarians can safely invest their savings in the stock market when the obligation to distribute wealth applies to institutions and not to individuals.

Now, is this what Rawls and liberals advocating principles of distributive justice are saying? Are they completely ignoring individual conduct while heralding the importance of "institutions?" And could they coherently do that given the well-known proposition that institutional performance is highly dependent on the way individual people behave?

In fact, Rawls invokes some virtues as necessary for the realization of a just society. Rawls argues that a "sense of justice" is one of the fundamental moral powers of citizens and essential to the stability of a just society.[8] These virtues "constitute a very great public good."[9] This is because just institutions would be constantly undermined unless we assume that citizens are committed to the institutions that they believe are just. A feature of the ideal of the just society is, in other words, the notion that people have a duty to "support and to comply with just institutions."[10]

Cohen argues that the idea of a sense of justice is beside the point. Cohen contends that the sense of justice represents an anomaly in Rawls' work because there seems to be no need for it. If justice is created by a just basic structure, it should not matter whether individuals are acting justly or not.[11] The premise of this objection is the one mentioned before: that if justice depends on the basic structure only, the extent to which citizens are virtuous must be irrelevant. Yet in this Cohen is likely to be wrong.

The purpose of the sense of justice in Rawls' vision is not that of maintaining *just distributions*—a task apparently allotted to the basic structure. Rather, the purpose of the sense of justice is that of maintaining the *basic structure*. The distinction between just distributions and a just basic structure must not be forgotten. A just basic structure promotes just distributions but is not identical to it.

Cohen does not consider the argument that institutions may need to be supported by virtues. This is why he misunderstands the important role that the sense of justice has to play in a just society. Rawls quite realistic claim is that, even when just distributions depend on institutional rather than individual choice, the institutions themselves may be distorted if people would constantly cheat on them. The sense of justice is meant to deal with exactly this problem. Citizens with a sense of justice will pay their taxes if they accept that the political institutions are just. Because they have a sense of justice they will "generally comply with these institutions."[12]

Although Cohen failed to appreciate this point I contend that his critique of Rawls still applies. It retains its force exactly because the sense of justice is not concerned with the promotion of just distributions. The issue raised by Cohen is not how to design just institutions but how to create just outcomes. The point that egalitarians could do a lot more to realize just outcomes, especially as long as our institutions are not just, is still effective against Rawls' political liberalism.

Two Objections

The claim that social justice depends on personal virtues of justice is likely to be contested for a number of familiar reasons. In particular there are two objections, of which Cohen is explicitly confronting only one, which may seem to have some initial plausibility. Here I will briefly refer Cohen's reply and a reply that could be given to the second objection.

The first objection explains the reluctance to recognize the virtues of justice by the fact that they matter so little causally. Patterns of wealth and income in modern societies depend almost entirely on the existing legal, political, and economic institutions and rules. Differences in the distribution of income between two countries, say Sweden and the United States, are explained by reference to existing taxes, rules of inheritance, and so on. The causal impact of egalitarian norms on patterns of income and distribution is presumably very small.[13] The exclusive focus on institutional issues by egalitarians is consequently quite justified.

The reply to this point is twofold. First, as Cohen makes clear, it is not always the case that the impact of individual acts of justice will be marginal or negligible. Individual contributions can affect the life of others immensely, although it is true that it affects only a restricted number of people. The lack of impact on the aggregate level does not imply that the impact of isolated acts of justice is insignificant for individuals.[14] Secondly, as I have argued above, it is hard to see why the greater efficiency of institutions is relevant, given that one lives in a society where institutions are not used for just purposes. It is one thing to say that you refrain from donating money because you *are* paying taxes that promote distributive justice more efficiently. It is quite another thing to say that you refrain from donating money because you *would like to*, though you presently do not, pay taxes to promote distributive justice. Now, giving nothing, neither collectively by taxes nor individually, could not be better than giving something.

The second objection concerns the psychological capacity of people. It holds that it would be utopian to require people to substitute the virtues of justice for their ordinary motivations concerning, for example, the welfare of friends and the family. As argued by Thomas Nagel and others, the existence of strong personal motivations (agent-relative reasons) is a fact and cannot be dispensed with—short of a revolution in human nature.[15]

Again we are faced with a point that, though it contains a grain of truth, is not strictly relevant. Nagel is asking what principles of justice can be justified. Given the premise that people cannot always be expected to be motivated by matters of justice, it may be reasonable to denounce theories that require citizens to attend constantly to the virtues of justice. But this is not the question we are asking. What we want to know is whether people who recognize egalitarian principles should evaluate their conduct by the same standards that apply to institutions. That is, the question is not *which* principles of social justice could be justified. We assume that you believe in the goodness of distributive justice and ask, instead, what this belief implies. It is perhaps "utopian" to hope that everyone, egalitarians and non-egalitarians alike, will recognize the virtues of justice in ordinary life. However, it cannot be utopian to hope that egalitarians would.

I do not believe, in sum, that these objections are successful in taking the edge off Cohen's thesis. They are not, because they do not dispute the picture of liberalism and liberal justice that Cohen is taking for granted. In fact, Cohen, as well as his critics, assumes that justice is the primary virtue of liberalism. Is it?

Ethical Liberalism

The premise of the discussion so far has been that liberalism is primarily a doctrine of justice. The picture is that liberals accept some principles of justice, but that they fail to adequately acknowledge the personal virtues and obligations entailed by them. Liberalism does not present the same high standards of justice to personal life as it does to political life. This is why Cohen believes that political liberalism is "incoherent."[16]

Rawls' theory may be vulnerable to this critique. Yet, it is a matter of much dispute whether Rawls' attitude to virtues is typically liberal. Numerous critics have argued that Rawls is exceptionally oblivious to the virtues traditionally associated with liberalism.[17] But if this criticism is justified, if Rawls neglects the importance of virtues in general, it is perhaps no surprise to find that he neglects the virtues of justice too. Thus, I suggest that we need to bring Cohen's charges face-to-face with ethical liberals who *do* recognize the importance of virtues. Only if it can be shown that they too ignore or are unable to accommodate the virtues of justice will we be in a position to conclude that Cohen has a point.

In fact, the narrow focus on the basic structure of society (and the consequent exclusion of virtues from political considerations) could be seen as a peculiar feature of political liberalism. Surely there are other varieties of liberal thought more hospitable to the idea of virtuous conduct. Possibly, these doctrines may not be as vulnerable to the charge of ignoring the virtues of justice. We consequently need to ask to what extent Cohen's critique applies even to what we may call "ethical" liberalism.

Ethical liberalism is not exclusively concerned with justice. Liberals through the ages have also been occupied with questions such as "how should one live?" Frequently, the liberal answer has been that the good life is to be found in the achievement of personal independence. To take one example, consider the wordings used by Bertrand Russell in identifying a liberal ethics:

> To abandon the struggle for private happiness, to expel all eagerness of temporary desire, to burn with passion for eternal things—this is emancipation, and this is the free man's worship.[18]

Russell illustrates the claim that to be a liberal is not merely to be concerned about the relations between citizens and the state. To be a liberal is also to adopt a particular lifestyle and to accept certain virtues as inherently desirable. Russell was to a considerable extent influenced by John Stuart Mill (who was his godfather), and Mill's concern with virtues is today widely recognized. Mill, just like Russell, believed that liberalism provided more than an outline for justice: it provided an account of the good life and its virtues.[19] Arguably, some of the most important liberal virtues are concerned with personal independence. From the point of view of ethical liberalism, the good life is inexorably bound up with the virtues of independence.

Now, how do Cohen's charges fare when confronted with ethical liberalism, for which the personal aspects of life are truly central? Cohen does not seem to confront ethical liberalism, although he deals with a standpoint that may appear to be related: the idea that the call for more virtues may infringe on people's right to "private space."[20] As Cohen notes, people might say that privacy gives you a right not to be virtuous. Admittedly, there is a sphere in which people are entitled to do whatever they want within the structure of the more general rules and laws of society. Given that there are such rights of privacy they may outweigh the demand to be virtuous.

Cohen makes it clear that he does not question the right to privacy as such. Rather, what matters is how we interpret privacy. Cohen's reply is essentially that people committed to distributive justice should reinterpret their idea of privacy so as to allow them to promote distributive justice more effectively by accepting standards of personal justice.[21] Given the urgency of social justice, the claim that egalitarians somewhat restrict their private sphere is scarcely unreasonable.

The point made by Cohen may borrow some support from a formal analysis of privacy rights. Such rights are likely to be what has been called "liberty rights."[22] That is, they protect us from having duties. Given that there is a right to privacy, it follows that there is a sphere in life in which I do not have duties to others. Thus, I have no duty to let you into my house and to show you my paintings. But because privacy is a liberty right, I may do these things if I want to. Given this observation, it appears that Cohen's reply was quite correct. If privacy is a liberty right, it is not violated if you decide to be more virtuous than you presently are.

The right to privacy, just as the virtues of independence, symbolizes the idea that personal relations and activities are of moral significance. But rights are different from virtues, and it is not clear what Cohen would say about liberals committed to the virtues of independence. I believe the issue is not resolved as easily as in the case of the right to privacy. This is so, because the virtues of independence are not "optional" in the same sense as privacy rights are. A person who believes that independence defines the good life could not accept Cohen's claim that recognizing the virtues of justice is simply a matter of choice. Choices that compromise personal independence will be costly in terms of the good life. Choices that compromise the right to privacy are not costly in that sense.

It turns out that the decisive issue concerns the relation between the virtues of justice and the virtues of independence. The issue concerns the potential conflict between the two sets of virtues. What we need to know is whether becoming more just will inevitably imply a loss of independence, or whether there is a way for ethical liberals to be coherently attached to both. Yet, before I attempt to answer this question we need to know more about the virtues of independence.

Two Conceptions of Personal Independence

What is personal independence? On one account, an independent person is someone without any ties or commitments. Independence implies solitude, isolation, and distance from social life. Independence thus conceived would be an ascetic ideal, perhaps not far from the lonely, silent, and simple life deep in the forests by the lake Walden, as described by Thoreau. Even more radically, personal independence may seem to require not only the absence of social commitments, but also the absence of commitments altogether. This is the extreme interpretation offered by another nineteenth-century writer, the nihilist Max Stirner. According to Stirner, the truly independent individual should not bind himself—or herself—to anyone or anything, i.e. not recognize duties even to oneself.[23]

These "solitary" conceptions of personal independence may seem demanding and perhaps not very attractive. Yet, whatever judgment we may pass on them, I believe they deviate from the liberal conception of personal independence. The defect of solitary independence is the assumption that life's value is determined by its shape, and not by the *way* it is shaped. Despite their many differences, both Thoreau and Stirner seemed to believe that independence is incompatible with social commitments. It did not matter to them how social commitments are made and accepted. Self-imposed commitments (as say, the choice to accept friendship) are as distortive to independence as are commitments that are more or less forced upon us (as say, accepting one's parents). The way you stand in relation to others is what eventually determines your degree of independence, whoever you are and whatever you happen to think. This, I believe, is the non-liberal feature of this notion of independence.

There is a different way to conceptualize personal independence that is more congenial to liberal purposes and aspirations. This is the idea of independence as concerned with the proper relation of the individual to the self—not to others. This ideal is conveyed in the familiar notions of autonomy and authenticity. Independence is achieved not by making life conform to a particular ideal of social relations, but by making life conform to our own ideal. This is shaping life rather than making life conform to a pre-defined shape. According to these ideals, independence no longer excludes social life and commitments. The important thing is *how* relations are accepted, not whether they are at all accepted.

Using a different terminology, we could say that autonomy and authenticity define independence in terms of second-order desires. The virtues of independence are realized when people accept and shape their own beliefs, desires, and preferences. The crucial thing is to want what you really want, to have desires that you really approve of, to prefer what you really would like to have. It is the conscious self-reflection on wants, the self-mastery of desires, that eventually makes a person independent.[24]

Liberal independence is about the mastery of the self. But as Diana Meyers points out, self-mastery involves both "self-direction" and "self-discovery."[25] The self has to be discovered before it can be directed. Unless you know yourself, unless your preferences form a coherent whole, you will be unable to act consistently. And unless you act consistently you will be unable to realize your autonomous or authentic self. Self-discovery is, in other words, a premise of both conceptions of personal independence. However, the ambiguity of "self-discovery" should not be underestimated. The self that independent people need to discover can be understood quite differently. Is it a self that speaks with one coherent voice, or is it a self that speaks in a natural voice too? In my view, in order to be autonomous, one needs only to create a coherent self, whereas authenticity loads the self with the qualities of being "natural" and "true."

Thus, the ideal of authenticity should be distinguished from the ideal of autonomy. In simple terms, the difference could be stated as the distinction between living the life *that is truly yours* and the life *that you really want*. The first view expresses an ideal of individual authenticity whereas the second view expresses an ideal of individual autonomy. Historically, these notions are found along somewhat different venues. Autonomy is associated with the enlightenment's belief in the sacredness of the individual and his or her rights.[26] Authenticity is associated with romanticism and the belief in the existence of a true, inner, self.[27]

The difference between authentic and autonomous independence is not historically well defined, though it is analytically quite clear. As we know now, both ideals accept as a crucial virtue the critical assessment of first-order desires (the things we want) in light of our deeper desires (the things we want to want). Where autonomy and authenticity differ is in the stories told about the content of second-order desires.

Believers in the ideal of authentic life accept the assumption that their second-order desires are somehow given by the structure of their personality or by nature. Thus, authenticity not only involves careful reflection on first-order wants and beliefs. Authenticity also includes the conviction that one's wants and beliefs should be shaped according to the "true self." There is, in this view, an inner voice that one should listen to. This voice is what finally determines what is valuable in one's life. Some people will believe that their authentic self is best realized in proximity to nature; others would find authenticity in a certain sexual or ideological orientation. But whatever is found at the bottom of the self, these desires are given by default, by birth, nature, or the social environment.

If, instead, you perceive the value of second-order reflection in terms of autonomy, you will not assume that any given activity is more natural than another. Autonomous people do not worry as much about the origin of second-order desires as they worry about using them. Recognizing autonomy as a liberal virtue entails that you value reflecting on your wants and examining the extent to which they are justified in the light of prior commitments and decisions. The autonomous person will aspire to act on first-order wants that are condoned by principles and commitments that have previously been accepted.[28]

Certainly, to assert that autonomy and authenticity are about the importance of second-order reflection is to some extent controversial. For instance, Bernard Berofsky argues that autonomy cannot be identified with second-order desires only.[29] According to Berofsky, second-order desires (e.g. reflective thinking) are not always more "important" or more "authentic" than those found in the first-order (e.g. love). Striving for autonomy, therefore, need not imply a preference for reflection rather than love.

Arguably, Berofsky correctly points out that autonomous people need not prefer the use of their second-order capacities to anything else—as long as this choice is itself autonomous. There is a sense in which it would be correct to say that you could autonomously choose to live a passionate rather than a reflective life.[30] However, Berofsky mistakenly assumes that autonomy is about achieving an authentic self. In my view, the ideals of authenticity and of autonomy are clearly distinct. This is illustrated by the fact that a person could autonomously choose to get rich rather than authentically.

The Virtue of Originality

There is a popular idea that it is a virtue to be "different." Arguably, the idea that it is good to strive for originality in character and lifestyle is familiar to many from everyday experience. In fact, this virtue is sometimes said to be typical of our liberal, individualist culture. The virtues of independence, whether understood in terms of autonomy or authenticity, are bound up with the value of difference and originality.

Yet there is something quite odd about striving always to be different. I believe Rousseau was right in remaining skeptical of this notion, which he described as the "fureur de se distinguer" in a derogatory way.[31] In fact, I argue that independence as originality is not a very liberal idea. The reason for this claim is similar to my objections in portraying the egoistic independence of Max Stirner as liberal. Thus, to believe that independence requires originality would—just as to believe that it requires solitude—amount to the view that the value of life depends on its shape rather than how it is shaped.

The distinct natures of originality and authenticity are seen by comparing the implications of these ideals. One person strives to be authentic, one person strives to be original—are they doing the same thing? A farmer, reflecting on the future, concludes that the rural life of his ancestors is the only "true one." The farmer may be living an authentic life, but is he original? An adolescent, seeking ways to receive respect, chooses to dress and talk like nobody else. The adolescent may be different, he may have originality—but is he authentic?

As I have argued, authenticity presupposes that some features of the self are immutable. Unless your self harbors second-order desires that you perceive as given, you will have no direction for the aim of becoming authentic. When you strive for originality the self must be seen as much more plastic. Originality involves comparisons with others and consequently the preparedness to amend and mold your self in the direction most likely to promote differences. A second point is that the belief in an authentic, "true" self need not involve the belief that this self is very much different from others. Authenticity requires neither distinctiveness nor originality, only that you remain faithful to your self. By contrast, accepting the value of originality you attach intrinsic value to difference or unorthodoxy. Thus originality, but not authenticity, calls for an unconditional break with conformity and convention.

The failure to appreciate this second point is common. For example, Charles Taylor asserts that "authenticity involves originality, it demands a revolt against convention."[32] Yet Taylor does not explain why authentic people have to be original and why authentic people are unable to accept convention. Taylor's critics similarly have a tendency to conflate originality and authenticity. According to Maeve Cook, the idea of authenticity is impracticable as a basis for a political theory since it rests on an utterly "unreliable and contentious" notion of "*unique* identity."[33] Cook believes that authenticity implies the need for recognizing "individual distinctiveness, understood as originality."[34] But in my view, to be an authentic person is to have first-order preferences that articulate your true second-order self. An authentic person need not differ from others, and there is no need, therefore, for him or her to be original.

So far I have attempted to demonstrate the distinction between authenticity and originality. I have not, however, demonstrated that originality is not a liberal virtue. After all, the value of originality seems widely recognized by liberals who, like John Stuart Mill and other individualists, denounced the life "in crowds." Mill disparaged people who did not think for themselves and who shunned "peculiarity of taste" as well as "eccentricity of conduct."[35] Apparently, Mill saw as "the chief danger of our time" the decline of eccentricity, and he therefore wished that there would be more signs of "originality" in society.[36] Thus it seems as if originality is an important virtue to liberals and therefore also for our society.

At the same time, others have described originality as nothing but a vice, as did Rousseau. The critique of originality is at the heart of his philosophy, because this idea seemed to him incompatible with the life of natural and uncivilized man.[37] Outside civilization, man lives alone and does not care for the opinions or conventions of others. In civilization man is sociable and strives for distinction, but only at the price of becoming dependent on the will of others. Considering this critique we realize that originality is an ambiguous ideal. Mill defended originality, even eccentricity, but he did not believe, as did Rousseau, that it would encourage conformity and dependence. Were they speaking about the same thing?

The assumption, so far, is that originality is the ideal of being like nobody else. It is a good feature of society, in this view, that people dress, eat, and think in distinctly different ways. The paradoxical feature of this idea, discerned by Rousseau, is that it leads to individual dependence on the conventions and habits of others. In order to distinguish yourself, e.g. in the way you dress and speak, you need to be very concerned with the way other people dress and speak.[38]

Perhaps originality can be understood differently, i.e. as the desire to ignore the opinions of others. To be original in this sense does not involve the urge to be different, exactly because this urge would imply attending to the opinions and conventions of others. Arguably, this is the kind of originality that Mill and Rousseau had in mind. They both feared conformity most of all, and saw independence in thinking (Mill) or will (Rousseau) as supremely important.[39]

Independence in thinking does not automatically provide anything such as unorthodox or original thoughts or habits. Thinking for yourself is no guarantee that you will end up thinking differently from others. Perhaps you will realize that you fancy the same thoughts and clothes as everybody else! Thus, the paradox of the second version of originality is that it may leave us far less "eccentric" than Mill would have preferred. Moreover, if thinking independently is all that originality means, its meaning is attenuated to the extent that it is indistinguishable from the idea of second-order reflection that unites both authenticity and autonomy. You certainly need to think for yourself in order to be either self-governing (autonomous) or true to your self (authentic). In this sense originality is clearly a prerequisite of any liberal vision of the good life—and presumably this is the message advanced by Mill and Rousseau.

It is high time to face the question we aimed at initially: Can the ideal of personal independence—understood either as autonomy or authenticity—be reconciled with the virtues of social justice?

Independence Modified?

Apparently, the ideals of authenticity and autonomy are compatible with a commitment to social justice. Autonomous people could choose to live by the virtues of justice as may, of course, authentic people. After all, the characteristic feature of the virtues of independence is that value is attached to individual choice. And the choices of individuals may certainly be concerned with the virtues of justice.

Yet, paradoxically, this view seems to attach too little importance to both independence and justice. Emphasizing the freedom to choose the virtues of justice ignores the extent to which justice may give rise to demands that restrict individual independence. As observed above, the virtues of justice may require great sacrifices and could consequently be costly in terms of personal independence. The virtues of authenticity and independence are not natural allies. As we can easily imagine, one's desire for shopping, or, less spectacularly, one's family commitments, may conflict with one's claims of desiring to support the poor and starving people of the world.

The image of choice also downplays the importance of justice. Perceiving the virtues of justice as purely a matter of choice is to degrade their moral salience. Choosing justice would seem to be no more inherently desirable than the choice of, say, climbing the Mount Everest by bike. There is evidently little to be said for the virtues of justice if they are neither better nor worse than the choice to become another Göran Kropp.

In that sense ethical liberalism seems to arrive at a position that is close to that of political liberalism. Reasoning from essentially different premises, they both conclude that the virtues of justice are "merely" a matter of individual choice. Liberalism "leaves room" for the virtues of justice but does not take seriously the possibility that there may be a strong connection between personal and political obligations to promote justice.[40]

One observation is that the argument connecting independence to justice needs to be "agent-relative." That is, the argument has to demonstrate why the virtues of justice are good for you and me, not merely why they are good "in general." The arguments usually provided for social justice are not like that; they are agent-neutral, designed to demonstrate the political necessity of justice. Although we have already conceded the political relevance of justice, we need to dig deeper in order to establish ethical reasons that are compatible with our commitment to the virtues of independence.

In his recent book, Alasdair MacIntyre argues that the "independent practical reasoner" achieves her ends primarily through social relationships. In order to establish relationships many virtues are required, among them the virtues of giving, receiving, and sharing. That is, a successful, independent person has to recognize that the virtues of justice are part of the good life.[41] This is not to say that the virtues of justice are accepted merely out of calculated self-interest. MacIntyre rejects that conclusion by noting that true social relationships assume uncalculated attitudes.[42] The life of the independent, practical reasoner therefore involves a just character rather than acts of justice.

A further attempt to link personal independence to the virtues of justice is provided by Ronald Dworkin. The value of personal independence is recognized by Dworkin as part of an ethical ideal, that of "life as a challenge."[43] As individuals, we have the power to give ourselves challenges, and the good life is one that allows us to meet these challenges appropriately. Independence thus understood is reminiscent of the ideals of autonomy and authenticity.[44] Now, it is a fact that each individual, in order to confront her challenges, needs a certain amount of resources. Whether one wants to be a fireman, a tennis player, or a monk, the challenge has certain costs. Thus, one needs to make judgments about the amount of resources one could legitimately expect in order to realize the good life. The ambition to live a good life will in other words inexorably raise issues concerned with distributive justice. Sorting out what justice means is "inescapably pertinent" for anyone pursuing the good life according to Dworkin.[45]

To achieve the virtues of independence, one needs social relationships (MacIntyre) and material resources (Dworkin). These goods are not just empirical prerequisites, but are conceptually bound up with the ideal of personal independence. They are perhaps best described as "constituent" goods.[46] Assuming that it makes sense to speak about a liberal vision of the good life, we may consequently conclude that this ideal is strongly associated with the virtues of justice. In sum, by recognizing the significance of virtues that are not institutional or political, ethical liberalism seems better equipped to meet the challenge of the egalitarian ethos presented by Cohen.

Notes

1. The Swedish prime minister, Göran Persson, defended Freivalds, saying that she acted as a "private person" and that he "understood" her choice to purchase public property given the "new rules." See Thomas Höjeberg, "Persson försvarar Freivalds," *Aftonbladet*, 28/08/2000. These were the same rules that Persson, Freivalds, and the Social Democratic Party were attempting to abolish.
2. Cohen's argument is found in a number of articles (notably Cohen, 1997). However, the bulk of the argument is summarized, and developed, in the book *If You're So Rich How Come You're an Egalitarian?* (Cohen, 2000) to which I will refer. For similar but distinct arguments about the importance of personal justice, see Smith, 1999 and Unger, 1995.
3. Cohen, 2000, p. 148.
4. See Beckman, 2001, chaps. 1, 3, and 4.
5. Rawls, 1971 and 1993; Barry, 1995.
6. Cohen, 2000, pp. 136f.
7. Murphy, 1998, p. 258.
8. Rawls, 1993, p. 16.
9. Rawls, 1993, p. 157.
10. Rawls, 1971, p. 115.
11. Cohen, 2000, p. 135.
12. Rawls, 1993, p. 141.
13. Williams, 1998.
14. In fact, as Scheffler argues, "it is often easier for us to overlook our causal contributions to those outcomes that are the joint result of the actions of many people." Scheffler, 2001, p. 39. And, as Roberto Unger argues, you can individually save up to thirty children's lives by donating $100 to organizations like UNICEF that constructs clean water facilities in the developing countries (Unger, 1995, p. 4).
15. Nagel, 1991, p. 93 and Estlund, 1998.
16. Cohen, 2000.
17. Galston, 1988; Berkowitz, 2000; and Beckman, 2001.
18. Russell, 1925, p. 55.
19. Berkowitz, 2000 and Clor, 1985. The claim that Mill represents a liberalism different from that criticized by Cohen borrows further support from the fact that Rawls, whom Cohen is turning against, explicitly contrasts his own position with that of Mill. Thus Rawls (1993, p. 199) writes, "political liberalism has a different aim [than] the liberalisms of Kant and Mill." In other words, the defects of Rawls' theory are unlikely to apply to Mill's thinking.
20. Cohen, 2000, p. 167.
21. Cohen, 2000, p. 168.
22. Jones, 1994, pp. 14ff.

23.   Leopold, 1995, p. xxii.
24.   "Strong evaluation" is the term used by Taylor (1989) to characterize this process. Cf. Frankfurt 1972.
25.   Meyers, 1989, p. 43.
26.   Larmore, 1996, pp. 127ff.
27.   Taylor, 1991.
28.   This picture of autonomy corresponds to the idea of autonomy as "moral legislation." Undoubtedly there are many other conceptions of autonomy, some of them describing autonomy as a way of life (see Hill, 1991, chap. 4.). Cf. Beauchamp (1991) who presents a list of eleven separate definitions of "autonomy."
29.   Berofsky, 1991, pp. 8 and 104.
30.   Cf. Dan-Cohen, 1992, p. 233.
31.   Manson, 1997, p. 44.
32.   Taylor, 1991, pp. 29 and 65.
33.   Cook, 1997, p. 271.
34.   Cook, 1997, p. 266.
35.   Mill, 1977, p. 265.
36.   Mill, 1977, p. 269.
37.   Wokler, 1997, p. 113.
38.   This view is reminiscent of Christopher Lash's description of the narcissist who "cannot live without an admiring audience" and for whom "the world is a mirror" rather than a place to shape to his own design. The logic of narcissism unravelled by Lash clearly resembles the conception of originality discussed here, and clearly has little to do with either authenticity or autonomy. Lash, 1978, p. 10.
39.   In fact, I believe the distinction between these conceptions of originality resolves what according to John Manson (1997) is a contradiction in Rousseau's writings. Rousseau proclaimed that he never wanted to be "original and act unlike others" but also that "I am not made like anyone else" (p. 46). Manson finds this confusing and concludes that Rousseau had "a desire to be original" (ibid.). Yet, it would be better to concede that Rousseau perhaps never strived to *be* original but that he was *thinking* independently and, as a result, might have *become* original.
40.   Cf. O'Neill, 1996, p. 142.
41.   MacIntyre, 1998, p. 120.
42.   MacIntyre, 1998, p. 121.
43.   Dworkin, 1990 and 2000.
44.   Thiébaut (1997) argues that Dworkin is typically a defender of personal autonomy. I do not think this is obvious. Dworkin stresses the particular character of each individual's "challenge" and thus hints on a theme typical to the tradition of authenticity.
45.   Dworkin, 2000, p. 264.
46.   Raz, 1986, p. 200.

6

Autonomy and Moral Responsibility:
On Virtues and the Common Good*

Göran Möller

Introduction

Our time is characterized by a view of freedom that stresses external freedom of action. Freedom is understood in the first instance in terms of negative freedom, that is to say, freedom from the interference of other people in the individual's own life. Being free is bound up with the idea that an individual may freely choose what values he or she should realize, as well as whatever social contexts he or she should become part of. To this latter domain belongs freedom in relation to such social commitments as might be a hindrance to realizing one's own plan of life.

This view of freedom also finds expression in political philosophy, being especially emphasized by libertarians such as Robert Nozick, though it is also held by many other liberal political philosophers. Freedom is to a high degree identified with the power to realize one's own desires so long as this does not infringe upon the freedom of others.[1] This view has even set its mark upon contemporary theology, so that here as well one has come to understand freedom in negative terms, with the consequence, among other things, that God's commandments become seen as incompatible with the freedom of the individual. The Lutheran theologian Reinhard Hütter writes:

> While in traditional Protestant ethics 'freedom and law' or the 'Christian life and God's commandments' were regarded as mutually dependent on and presupposing each other, they have increasingly become mutually exclusive in modern Protestant ethics...[2]

* This essay was translated by Stephen Theron.

The important question concerning what is needed for a person to develop into an independent moral subject is, on the other hand, seldom raised. One disregards the aspect of freedom having to do with how an individual needs to be formed by a societal environment if he or she is to develop into an autonomous subject, able to assume responsibility for his or her actions. For freedom is not only formal. It is also substantial. If our freedom is to be meaningful, we need to acquire the ability to judge between different values, to determine what our priorities shall be among these values, and then to realize them in our actions. This all presupposes that we acquire various virtues.

We acquire virtues within different communities and social networks in general. The virtues have to exist within the various social structures before they can be transferred to new human beings. In this connection Alasdair MacIntyre speaks of relationships of giving and receiving.[3] We depend upon such structures both for the acquisition of virtues and for their maintenance and further development. The purpose of this article is partly to discuss how individual good in the form of freedom and the realization of a good life is dependent upon some common good in the form of virtues and various structures of giving and receiving, and partly to discuss how this dependence entails a responsibility for the maintenance of these structures.

Virtues are complex phenomena, not subject to exhaustive characterization in any single conceptual definition. As a point of departure I will, nonetheless, employ the definition formulated by Alasdair MacIntyre in *After Virtue*.

> The virtues...are to be understood as those dispositions which will not only sustain practices and enable us to achieve the goods internal to practices, but which will also sustain us in the relevant kind of quest for the good, by enabling us to overcome the harms, dangers, temptations and distractions which we encounter, and which will furnish us with increasing self-knowledge and increasing knowledge of the good.[4]

Virtues are Needed so as to be Able to Realize the Good

Let me begin by inquiring how the virtues might be a precondition for realizing the good from the perspective of the private individual. Following MacIntyre, I shall distinguish between four different kinds of goodness. Thus there is, firstly, a type of goodness having to do with the well-being we experience when various sorts of needs are satisfied—hunger, thirst, or sexual desire, for example.[5] We tend to strive spontaneously and without reflection to satisfy desires of this kind.

A second form of goodness is found in the various values we can learn to realize within us through practices of various types.[6] This is a goodness enabling us to develop various potentialities within ourselves. We can do this within the private sphere, in our professional life, or through various leisure activities. To become an accomplished workman, nurse, or journalist implies contributing to the realization of different values common to a given profession and workplace, but simultaneously enriching the individual concerned, since he or she thereby develops his own potentialities and participates with others in various worthy achievements.

A third kind of goodness attaches to whatever is good as a means to something else.[7] Even what is good in itself can have such a simultaneous instrumental value. This applies to our work, for example. Besides ministering to various intrinsic values work supplies our needs, enabling us to realize other values as well. Through our work, moreover, we can contribute to the good of others in various ways.

A fourth aspect of goodness concerns the good life as lived by the individual, which entails relating different kinds of goods or values to one another in an individual life so as to achieve thereby a good life as a whole.[8] It is a matter of finding a right combination of different kinds of goods through, for example, reconciling conflicting roles and interests with one another. As MacIntyre shows, it is characteristically human to be able to deliberate concerning what is good and, from the choice one makes in consequence of such reflection, to give one's life a certain direction. To have such a capacity implies, in MacIntyre's terminology, that one is an "independent practical reasoner." This capacity is a prerequisite for the ability to live an integrally good life or, in other words, to flourish. MacIntyre refers here to the Aristotelian conception of *eudaemonia*.

What significance do the virtues have in relation to realizing the good? Firstly, they are a precondition for setting the right limits to our pursuit of the first type of good mentioned. For the small child, satisfaction of basic needs is at the center of everything. Later, however, he or she learns to discipline this drive to immediately satisfy his or her various needs, partly because he or she learns to consider others, partly because he or she learns to question some of his or her spontaneous urges in order to do justice to other needs and values both in the short and long term. This can be described as the child's acquiring a capacity to distinguish between two types of desires, viz. "first-order" and "second-order" desires. First-order desires are those where we want spontaneously to do different things and get different needs satisfied. Second-order desires, on the other hand, have our will itself and its desires as object and thus call for a quantitative and qualitative discrimination between different desires and impulses.[9] That we sometimes need to question and even restrain our spontaneous desires in no way suggests, however, that doing justice to our different needs is not an important element in the embodiment of a good life.

Moreover, virtues are a precondition for maintaining those practices desirable in society as enshrining various goods of intrinsic value. Among other things, the virtues enable us to fulfill the various roles demanded by such practices.

Even this very ability to reflect upon the different kinds of goodness to be found in life—an ability marking out "an independent practical reasoner"—is an expression of a virtue, is an aspect, namely, of the cardinal virtue of *phronesis*. Human potentialities are susceptible to development in widely varying ways in different contexts. What remains the same for an independent practical reasoner in all these contexts, however, is the ability to make independent choices based on discrimination between the various goods or benefits to be gained. MacIntyre writes:

> What it is for human beings to flourish does of course vary from context to context, but in every context it is as someone exercises in a relevant way the capacities of an independent practical reasoner that her or his potentialities for flourishing in a specifically human way are developed. So if we want to understand how it is good for humans to live, we need to know what it is to be excellent as an independent practical reasoner, that is, what the virtues of independent practical reasoning are.[10]

How Virtues Make Freedom Possible

How are the virtues related to human freedom? Let me begin by mentioning some conditions that need to be filled for a person to qualify as an autonomous subject. The aspect of freedom most emphasized in our time is the need, in order to be free, of having a certain degree of scope for individual action through an absence of external hindrances to what one would do. One usually calls this aspect of freedom "negative freedom," which bespeaks a freedom *from* other people's interference in one's life. This aspect has sometimes been understood as both a necessary and a sufficient condition for freedom.

There are also, however, other aspects to freedom that are important. Thus one must be able, to be free, to govern one's behavior in accordance with certain overarching purposes, goals, and ideals. One should, in other words, be able to formulate second-order desires and to let one's will be formed by them. This is a freedom that a person has in relation to himself. For autonomous behavior is not haphazard and arbitrary. On the contrary it is behavior inserted into a context of purpose. We exclude voluntarily certain possible behavioral alternatives just because they are incompatible with certain controlling goals that we have in our lives or with those ideals and principles which we want to characterize us as human beings. This implies, among other things, a control over our spontaneous impulses. One who cannot control his impulses is scarcely free, and it is with the help of the virtues that we can govern and control ourselves.

We further need, for our freedom to have direction, to have some meaningful alternatives among which to choose. This presumes that we have first been formed and have developed in a given tradition and have indeed participated in various types of corresponding activities. We must be able to develop our potentialities in such a way as makes it possible to realize what we want to do and even become conscious of other possibilities. This aspect of freedom is usually called "positive freedom." Let me give a trivial example: one who has never learned to play the piano can certainly strike the keys as he sees fit, but it is of course pointless. For a musical performance to be possible we must have acquired the ability to play. Thus, in general, we must have been formed by an environment if we are to be free in a meaningful way.

Finally, the power to reflect over how one wants to shape one's life is itself a further aspect of freedom. To make such decisions on the basis of independent, reflective inquiry into what one values, which is typical of an independent practical reasoner, is an important aspect of freedom. What degree of freedom people attain in this matter of shaping one's own life in different ways naturally varies immeasurably between different cultures and societies or between different social levels in one and the same society. The power to make independent and reflective choices is, however, something that distinguishes a person who is free in different contexts, even if the room for maneuver is sometimes very limited.

Structures of Giving and Receiving

What is needed, then, from his or her surroundings for a person to be able to acquire various virtues? The virtues must exist in a social context before they can be appropriated by private individuals, since we acquire virtues in accordance with a pattern supplied by others. There must therefore be a social structure involving parents, teachers, and others who have themselves acquired both the virtues they will mediate to their charges and those virtues needed for responsible care and indeed for mediating all kinds of abilities, including virtues over again.

To become conscious both of our strong sides and of our limitations we need people in our environment who, with honesty and straightforwardness, make clear to us both our strengths and our weaknesses in a way that does not oppress but rather helps us to develop. Living a good life requires also that we possess self-reliance in function of our self-image and our self-confidence in general. Even for this we depend upon our environment, not least upon those persons who are especially close to us and mean a lot to us. Such people should be equipped with virtues like honesty and love.

This brief sketch should serve to show the many-faceted social structure that is required as a background for anyone to be able to achieve a good life. It should also help to bring out how even the environment needs to be marked by different kinds of virtues if such a development is to be at all possible. MacIntyre speaks of networks of giving and receiving. These networks reach far beyond the time-frame of an individual human life. When a person is born, then, if all goes well, he or she is taken into and formed by a social milieu typified by such structures. The person can then later contribute, according to the measure of his ability, to maintaining this structure.[11]

These networks of giving and receiving are thus a precondition for our being able to develop into independent practical reasoners. This does not imply, however, that we will be able to manage on our own once we have reached a certain level of development. To be able to keep this power alive, as also to develop it further, we need throughout our lives to have various kinds of support from our surroundings. This depends partly upon the fact that our development is never finally perfected, partly upon the continuous need, if we are to achieve self-knowledge and self-awareness, for different kinds of environmental feedback. Besides this we need help from others to correct our various errors, be they intellectual or moral. We can get this help in our professional lives from colleagues or work mates, and in private life from our family and friends.[12]

Thus the virtues make it possible for us to achieve a good life, partly because, with their help, we have the power to reflect over what is good, partly because they make it possible for us to realize such a good in cooperation with others in different social contexts. MacIntyre writes:

> ...the virtues [enable] us to become independent practical reasoners, just because they also enable us to participate in relationships of giving and receiving through which our ends as practical reasoners are to be achieved...[13]

Common Responsibility

Virtues can be characterized as "common goods." Common goods or, put differently, "irreducible social goods," in a society are such goods as cannot be good for an individual person if they are not also good for others.[14] Phenomena typically adduced as examples of common goods are language and historical memory. As we saw above, the virtues are in many different ways a precondition for each of us to be able to realize his or her individual good. For acquiring the virtues, however, we remain dependent upon their being mediated to us by our environment. It is through the various networks of giving and receiving that such a transference is possible. We depend upon these structures for the realization of our own good. At the same time we can contribute to the maintenance of such structures through our own varied social cooperation.

It is in our own interest that the structures we depend upon be upheld. At certain stages of our lives we are more especially dependent upon the support of other people, not least when we are children, but also in times of sickness, through some handicap, or when we are growing old. MacIntyre writes:

> So each of us achieves our good only if and insofar as others make our good their good by helping us through periods of disability to become ourselves the kind of human being...who makes the good of others her or his good, and this not because we have calculated that, only if we help others, will they help us, in some trading of advantage for advantage.[15]

For the system to function integrally, there needs to be not only takers, but givers. We have, therefore, a moral responsibility to give something back during those stages of our lives in which we can be active. This giving as debt to others cannot function reciprocally in the sense that we give back in the same way and to the same persons from whom we have received. It is, however, possible to give back in a transferred sense, for example through repaying what we received as children by caring for one's own children or for others in need of our support. According to MacIntyre, there exists a kind of implicit moral demand for such repayment. Some people's ability to give back in this way is more limited, especially if they are severely handicapped and thus continuously dependent on others. Yet these people can often contribute to their neighbors' good in other ways.[16]

It needs to be emphasized, however, that the help of various kinds that we can give to others can simultaneously enrich our own lives. If we are too absolute in distinguishing between actions aiming to promote our own good and those intended to benefit others then we miss an important aspect of the common good, viz. that it can have several subjects simultaneously. Here we encounter what is also an important aspect of the virtues: that to act in accordance with a virtue such as generosity, for example, can be a good both for the giver and for the receiver. MacIntyre writes:

> To assert of a given action that it was performed for its own sake is not at all incompatible with saying of that same action that it was performed for the sake of that individual or these individuals to whose good it was directed. So acts of generosity, justice, and compassion are done for the sake of others and are worth doing in and for themselves.[17]

What we are saying is fully in accordance with the Aristotelian notion that the good life consists in the practice of the virtues.

A conclusion one may draw from the above is that it is not possible to entirely separate a single person's individual good from what is good for other people or from the common good in a society, and that there exists a common responsibility in society for maintaining the structures through which both the individual and common good can equally be realized.

Notes

1.   Important exceptions to this characterization include, among others, Joseph Raz and Charles Taylor. See Raz, 1986 and Taylor, 1985 and 1995.

2.   Hütter, 1998, p. 37.
3.   MacIntyre, 1999, p. 120.
4.   MacIntyre, 1981, p. 219.
5.   MacIntyre, 1999, p. 68.
6.   Ibid., p. 66.
7.   Ibid.
8.   Ibid., p. 66f.
9.   For the distinction between "first-order" and "second-order" desires, see Frankfurt, 1988.
10. MacIntyre, 1999, p. 77.
11. Ibid., p. 99-108.
12. Ibid., p. 96.
13. Ibid., p. 120.
14. Ibid., p. 119.
15. Ibid., p. 108.
16. Ibid., p. 100f.
17. Ibid., p. 112.

7

The Politics of Virtue in the French Revolution

Ruth Scurr

The eighteenth-century feminist and philosopher, Mary Wollstone-craft, regretted that she had not traveled more widely before she arrived in France in 1792. She thought that if only she had already been familiar with less developed societies like Denmark, she would have taken a very different view of the French during those revolutionary years. With hindsight she believed that what happened in France at that point depended directly upon the degree of sophistication that French society in general had then reached. The "virtues of a nation bear an exact proportion to their scientific improvements."[1] Wollstonecraft saw a strong general connection between scientific advancement and social virtue. She also had a strikingly positive and sanguine interpretation of the French Revolution as the embodiment of advances in both science and morality. On the strength of this vision she proposed a new model for the eighteenth-century Grand Tour. Those who traveled to complete a liberal education should begin in the northern states and progress to the more polished or advanced parts of Europe. The point was not to look backwards to classical antiquity or the life of the noble savage, but to look forwards instead, with an eye to the evolution of society.

It is very easy to dismiss Mary Wollstonecraft. How could anyone be so optimistic about the relationship between science and virtue? How could someone who had been in Paris as the Terror was beginning, and had seen her friends and political heroes arrested on charges of hypocrisy, possibly think that the French Revolution was straightforwardly progressive?[2] But there is a sense in which Wollstonecraft was right and her optimism resonates with our own. As outsiders, or as citizens, we too expect more from economically advanced societies: more individual freedom, more collective virtue, and more sophisticated institutional mechanisms for handling the relations between the two. Where Wollstonecraft was wrong was in supposing that the French Revolution was a straightforward example of scientific and moral advance. Arguably, it may have been so at its outset. But in a very short time the Revolution eroded the distinction between education and indoctrination that was so precious to moderate revolutionaries like Condorcet, and set out on the project of regenerating the French people to make them worthy of the new republic they were to receive. In this way independence was attacked in the name of virtue. One of the reasons that the French Revolution casts so much light on the relationship between individuality, virtue, and collective life is that it spans the decline of apparently progressive social aspirations into unmistakable terror and indoctrination. The speed of this decline was dramatic and extreme. This might make the French Revolution seem remote from our contemporary concerns with virtue inside stable and prosperous representative democracies. However, if we remember Mary Wollstonecraft's ill-considered optimism, and stop to consider less economically, socially, and politically stable states than our own, it becomes very clear that, if we are to understand our own advantages better, we first need to know what they are grounded in.

The concept of virtue played a notorious and important role during the French Revolution. Initially, the events of 1789 defined the nation (the legitimate possessor of popular sovereignty and the only source of true constituting power), in opposition to aristocratic privilege and corruption, a milieu of evident vice. But as the Revolution proceeded, the alleged presence or absence of virtue became a means to make further (and increasingly arbitrary) distinctions between the Revolution's friends and enemies. Its so-called enemies were accused of simulating virtue. But nothing was more likely to prompt simulation of virtue than its role in distinguishing friend from enemy, in the midst of the Terror, and in the face of the imminent prospect of the Guillotine. The initial negative definition of the nation's friends (those who were not privileged or free-riding on the hard work of the Third Estate) gave way to a positive definition of virtue itself, where this could mean anything that those with power decided. This account has long been presented as an explanation of the causes of the Revolutionary Terror. It is a pattern that was to repeat itself many times in subsequent revolutions.

In his recent account of Jacobinism, the Harvard historian of the French Revolution, Patrice Higonnet, has attempted to rescue virtue from the stigma of having precipitated the Terror and restore more positive connotations to its role within the Revolution.[3] Higonnet acknowledges that Jacobinism evolved rapidly during the early revolutionary years, from 1789 to the fall of Robespierre in 1794—the membership, ideas, and politics of the Jacobin clubs were far from continuous during these years. But he identifies a continuous structure of preoccupation at the center of Jacobin ideology, and with deliberate anachronism characterizes this by its dual commitment both to individualism and to communitarianism:

> Jacobinism's doubled message was of individual becoming and altruistic involvement. Its core belief was that mankind could best realize its true self in the politicized context of a universalist republic.[4]

Higonnet argues that individualist, or autonomy-regarding, priorities on the Jacobin agenda (the destruction of feudalism, the declaration of rights, the extension of the franchise) were always in tension with communal, or other-regarding, priorities (the general will, the public good, and the nation). This tension, he argues, was sustainable but necessarily unstable. On this account, communitarian priorities gained ascendancy over individualist priorities, and then issued naturally, if not ineluctably, in terrorism. Higonnet's point is to insist that the decline into Terror was contingent and historically prompted, not an inevitable emanation from Jacobin politics. For this reason, "Jacobinism can still be a model for modern democrats." Like us, the Jacobins were aware of the tension between individual autonomy and the indispensable role of virtue in generating the social cohesion on which all societies depend, and democracies most of all.[5]

It is not necessary to accept a strong version of the flamboyant, and in many respects obviously inappropriate, claim that Jacobinism offers a model to modern democrats. A weaker version is more instructive: namely, that Jacobinism highlighted many of the concerns that have remained prominent in modern democracies and contemporary political theory. But insofar as it inadvertently highlighted the tension between individualism and communitarianism well in advance of contemporary political theorists (such as Charles Taylor,

John Rawls, and Jürgen Habermas), it did so only in part because of any freestanding ideas about the structure and prerequisites of modern society. As a political movement and a body of opinion, Jacobinism was a perpetually revised series of reactions to the events of the French Revolution. It emerged and developed alongside a wealth of competing responses to these same, dramatic and historically consequential events. The fact that Jacobinism reflects some of the challenges that face modern democrats is a product of the wider fact that the French Revolution itself involved the birth of the modern representative republic in Europe.[6]

It is more the scope and urgency of reflections on virtue during the French Revolution than the use of this concept by any particular set of political actors that illuminates our contemporary concerns with the relations between individual and collective virtues. What is important is less the Revolutionaries' competing definitions of virtue (or the virtues) than the role they assigned to it in explaining and promoting social coherence. We need first to register the key contrast between internal and external perspectives on virtue. An internal perspective focuses on the subjective struggle of particular individuals to live the good life. Political virtue in this respect requires citizens to possess and exhibit the capacity for disinterested dedication to their political community. In eighteenth-century France there was an extremely rich variety of thinking about the psychological and social basis of virtue. Retrospectively, scholars have identified a Commonwealth ideology, focused on virtue in the political domain and on the potentially corrupting impact of commerce and luxury upon it.[7] But these concerns were shared by a much wider array of writers (such as Montesquieu, Mably, and Rousseau).[8] Rousseauist appeals to the integrity of the upright heart also overlapped to a certain extent with both Jansenist and patriotic preoccupations.[9] Traditional Christian theological and moral virtues were emphasized in the branch of Jesuit thinking known as Molinism, which defended the legitimacy of the authority of both Church and State, and offered a very optimistic assessment of human nature's capacity for virtue.[10] After 1789, as the Revolution continued to unfold, the internal perspective on virtue became even more politically prominent.[11] Jacobins, as Higonnet has shown, conceived the virtuous life as above all an exacting, ongoing struggle, requiring perpetual vigilance over the motivations and actions of self and others.[12] This intense focus on individual aspiration and personal failure in the course of political struggle was inherently disruptive. It had little imaginatively in common with soberer inquiries into the conditions, processes, and institutions that favored the development of some forms of behavior or dispositions, and curtailed others. For this externalized perspective on virtue, social cooperation, political stability, or the communal good resulted not from individual spiritual triumph, but from predictable social and economic dynamics, or from the acquisition of learnt skills imparted (directly or indirectly) by the state to its dependent citizens.

The relations between these two perspectives on virtue—the internal and the external—in the thinking of individual Revolutionaries are too extensive and too intricate to treat here. Instead, we consider a much narrower but equally significant topic: the surprising consensus among individuals from very different persuasions on the need for social institutions to foster political virtue. Across a broad spectrum of political conviction the leading intellectual interpreters of the Revolution's requirements agreed that institutions designed to mold individuals for collective social life were an indispensable component of the modern republic. The search for a form of virtue suited to a large commercial state such as France, and capable of providing collective stability for its individual citizens, underpinned the formal constitutional struggles between 1789 and the construction of Napoléon's Empire. Whilst several other conceptions of the sources of the social and political virtues were present and influential in the epoch before the Revolution, it was above all Montesquieu's work that shaped the subsequent development of revolutionary reflections on these sources. This prominence stemmed from his emphasis on the specifically political role of virtue in sustaining a republican form of government. On the eve of the Revolution, Montesquieu's typology of three drastically contrasted regime types was still the most influential framework through which to consider the role of virtue in government, society, and economy.[13] After the declaration of the republic in 1792, the revolutionaries needed to identify for themselves the virtues capable of sustaining a modern as opposed to an ancient republic. Four theorists played roles of particular importance in these discussions: Condorcet and Brissot from the so-called Girondin faction, and Robespierre and Saint-Just from the Jacobin Club.[14] Despite their bitter factional animosities, these intensely politically responsive individuals were at one in acknowledging the role of virtue in molding citizens for collective life.

On Montesquieu's account, the three regimes of republican, monarchical, and despotic government are sustained, respectively, by the principles of virtue, honor, and fear.[15] Virtue in a republic is defined as the love of the republic, a product of feeling rather than of knowledge. Montesquieu describes the virtues that sustain republics but are redundant inside monarchies in heroic terms: "love of the homeland, desire for true glory, self-renunciation, sacrifice of one's dearest interests, and all those heroic virtues we find in the ancients and know only by hearsay."[16] These virtues are redundant inside monarchies, he argues, because here laws replace them. Virtue is not unknown under a monarchical form of government, but it is rare, frequently ridiculed, and certainly not the spring or principle of action that sustains the regime itself. Instead, monarchies rely upon the principle of honor, and individual prejudice replaces political virtue. Taken together, the laws and individual prejudice inside a monarchy can have the same political consequences as virtue operating inside a republic. Neither honor nor laws are present in despotic states, where men are equal, because all are in some measure slaves, and none can rely on a fixed code of law or constitution. Hence, fear is the principle of this form of government.

The revolutionaries of 1789 had no intention of establishing a republic in France, nor did they believe it possible to do anything of the kind. Between 1789 and 1791 the National Assembly struggled, virtually without a single dissident voice, to design a constitutional monarchy for France. But even before this struggle had proved futile and resulted in the hasty declaration of a republic in 1792, the principle of honor was strongly contested. Honor, on Montesquieu's account, relied upon clear and graduated distinctions of ranks among the people. Honor required preferences and distinctions, and even a hereditary nobility. Yet the claims of the Third Estate to embody the nation—the establishment of the principles of popular sovereignty and equality of right, followed by the formal declaration of rights— were irreconcilably at odds with preserving the principle of honor. Statesman and intellectual Jacques Necker saw this and tried to encourage the National Assembly to rescue a reformed, less provocative version of the distinction of ranks that had existed under the *ancien régime*.[17] Following Montesquieu, he argued that the proposed constitutional monarchy could not function in the absence of any such hierarchical structures. The only alternative to this that Necker saw (though he did not himself advocate it) was a genuinely republican form of government operating on the entirely different principle of virtue.

Once the republic was declared in 1792, the question of publicly orientated virtue and its role inside republican regimes moved to the center of political and constitutional discussion. What were the causal antecedents of public virtue? What was its political significance? How was virtue possible at all in a modern rather than ancient republic? Was virtue essential to a social framework that gave individuals both the opportunity to become autonomous and the opportunity to exercise their autonomy? The historical answers to these questions reflect the relative importance that different revolutionary thinkers gave to spontaneous sociability and coercive institutions in maintaining social cohesion. It is in the relation between these two that the concepts of virtue and autonomy, dependence and independence become prominent.

* * *

In 1786, three years before the French Revolution, Condorcet defined republicanism in terms of legal recourse against the decisions of the political power.[18] He defined law in terms of truth rationally deduced from the principles of natural law. There is a strong contrast here with Rousseau's definition of the law as the genuine expression of the general will, and with even more open-ended and democratic understandings of the law as the will of the people, or the majority of the people, or the majority of the people's representatives. The republicanism that Condorcet developed during the early years of the French Revolution and openly professed in 1791 relied heavily upon political rationalism: the expectation that reason could and should play a significant role throughout the political sphere. Hence, at the same time as he advocated universal suffrage, Condorcet also proposed a council to sit alongside the legislative body, overseeing the formation of its laws and providing essential guidance.[19] Understanding was set above feeling, and Montesquieu's definition of virtue inside a republic, where love of the fatherland was the product of feeling rather than knowledge, was implicitly rejected.

Condorcet's reassessment of the role of virtue inside the modern republic did not go unnoticed. During the constitutional debates of 1793, as the Convention strove to give form and content to the new republic, Condorcet hoped that his elaborate educational plan would at last be instituted.[20] But when he came to present his plan he was immediately attacked and accused (by Durand Maillane) of placing science (or reason) above virtue. This prompted sharp debate over whether it is more important for citizens to love or understand the laws, and which of these two outcomes should form the center of the nation's educational aspirations. The hierarchical aspects of Condorcet's proposals, which culminated in the National Society of Arts and Sciences, an elite body with overall responsibility for the entire system of education, were criticized as a clear violation of republican equality. In the course of this debate one deputy to the Convention (Rabaut de Saint-Etienne) drew the key distinction between enlightenment and virtue, arguing that national regeneration really required a revolutionary cult that could foster virtue and the feelings upon which it depended.[21] For Condorcet this was to ignore the distinction between education and indoctrination, and he rejected entirely the claim that the Revolution's future and the fate of France could depend on a policy of public indoctrination.

* * *

Brissot belonged to the same broad political group as Condorcet (the Girondins), and he shared the latter's rationalist definition of the law. He defined the republic itself as a government in which all powers were either delegated or representative, elected by and for the people, and temporary or removable.[22] Like many of his contemporaries (and the Abbé Sieyès most especially), he relied upon the concept of representation to distinguish republicanism from direct democracy.[23] But he continued to stress the need to explore and promote the public interest beyond the representative sphere. He argued "...that there is never an end to debate amongst free people; that liberty cannot exist but by debate; [and] that silence announces its extinction."[24] But whilst the political powers would be tempered by public opinion, in turn public opinion would be moderated by the "tutors of the people." When it came to explaining how social cohesion could be sustained in a society free from repressive political force, Brissot fell back upon the idea of virtue. Whilst he sought to present the representative system as a substitute (under modern conditions), for the absence of the virtues that sustained classical (unlike modern) republics, the role of virtue was retained in his recognition that the preservation of liberty required the development of morality amongst the people. Whereas Condorcet hoped to extend the competence of the citizen and so minimize the need for both repressive force and public indoctrination, Brissot ended up relying on the latter very heavily. The frank acknowledgment that virtue was required to bridge the gap between the individual and social cohesion inside large commercial states linked him to his immediate political enemies, Robespierre and Saint-Just. The attempt to design institutions to foster social cooperation was one way to avoid direct coercion of individuals by their governors; but it was still a form of indirect coercion, opening up avenues through which the state could treat its citizens as patients in need of a cure. By 1793 both Robespierre and Saint-Just were convinced that the cure France required was their own particular version of republican government, and that any citizens who rejected this remedy should be reformed or eradicated. Robespierre and Saint-Just had a model of social cohesion that they sought to apply to individuals in real historical time. This inverted the approach of Condorcet, Brissot, and others who tried to understand how individuals spontaneously cooperate, and to improve upon this with state institutions and coercion only as and where these were clearly required. Even so, the two sides in this debate are rather too close for comfort.

* * *

In contrast to Brissot, whose premise was the absence of classical virtues from the modern republic, Robespierre derived all of his major political principles from the idea of political virtue (virtue at the core of politics itself). In the years between 1789 and the official declaration of the first French republic in 1792, Robespierre insisted that government must be based on ethical principles, that the people as such is good, and that in every community there must be a single sovereign will.[25] Echoing Montesquieu, he defined virtue as *L'amour de la patrie*, a psychological disposition that identified public with private interests. *Patrie* he equated with the sovereignty of the people, and with equality of right. In this respect, Robespierre offers a clear example of the dual structure of Jacobin priorities, as Patrice Higonnet analyzes it. Robespierre was an individualist in envisaging equality of right and the possibility of giving this institutional effect as vital components of popular sovereignty. During the early revolutionary years he had headed the campaign for democratic sovereignty, insisting that talent, virtue, and success in free elections were the only necessary qualifications for membership of a genuinely representative assembly. But he was also a universalist in seeing virtue as requiring the identification of public and private interests and submission to the will of all (a more practical, if adulterated substitute for the General Will as this had been theorized by Rousseau).

Although the concept of virtue played such a prominent role in Robespierre's thinking, he was neither one of the earliest, nor one of the most elaborate theorists of a republican form of government. He considered the terms monarchy and republic vague, and the contrast between them elusive. He also thought that a republic, in the sense of a state in which the public interest predominated and was not appropriated by a self-serving elite, was compatible with a monarchical form of government. Although Robespierre was critical of the powers left to Louis XVI under the constitutional monarchy of 1791, he defended the new constitution for most of its short life, months after Brissot and Condorcet called openly for a republic. There were tactical reasons for this. Robespierre and Brissot had clashed bitterly at the Jacobin Club over the question of foreign war, and as late as May 1792 Robespierre was still hoping to discredit his Brissotin opponents by saddling them with the still contentious label of republicanism. But it is also important to emphasize that insofar as Robespierre was a leading and impassioned proponent of the politics of virtue early in the Revolution, this did not involve him in any deep or sustained thinking about the functioning of government. Towards institutionalized power and authority he was still suspicious and contestatory, rather than preoccupied with the practicalities of reform. He followed Rousseau in insisting on the complete subordination of the executive to the legislative power, and in equating sovereignty with the rule of law. During his ardent campaign for individual liberties in the National Assembly (1789–1791), Robespierre displayed no awareness of potential conflict between individual liberties and popular sovereignty, and no understanding of the role that political institutions might play in reconciling these two. Importantly, this position was neither unique to Robespierre, nor unusual.

When he became a leading member of the Revolutionary Government in 1793, Robespierre had to change abruptly.[26] From being one of authority's fiercest critics, he was now one of its strongest advocates. He renounced the principle of the separation of powers and the subordination of the executive, arguing that ministers were no longer chosen by the king, but servants of the (recently purged) Convention. Whilst the people might rule by virtue during ordinary times, during a revolution virtue must be supplemented by Terror, and Terror must emanate from virtue, providing "prompt, severe and inflexible" justice.[27] He stressed the need for government to exercise tight control over the people's opinions, and he abandoned the liberty of the press. In July 1793 he turned to education, arguing that it was necessary to bring about a complete regeneration of the people. He proposed that *la patrie* should take infants at the age of five from their parents, returning them to society at the age of twelve, already fully trained and worthy citizens of the republic.[28] Later still he echoed Montesquieu's analysis of virtue, pointing out that under monarchy only the king needed to be virtuous and love the *patrie*, and similarly, under aristocracy it was enough if the elite families displayed civic virtue. But in a democracy where the state was truly the *patrie* of all, every individual must love it.

* * *

The familiar revolutionary trajectory of Robespierre's thinking was even more precipitate in the case of Saint-Just, who vacillated between virtual anarchy and a schoolmaster state.[29] On the one hand, he affirmed the emergence of individual rights inside the modern republic, in contrast to their marked absence in the ancient republics of Athens and Sparta. On the other, he lamented the decline in patriotism and the rise of self-love, egoism, or private interest concomitant with individual rights. Unlike Robespierre, he was fascinated by the role for political institutions to reconcile individual with public interest. Before the nature and consequences of Saint-Just's plethora of republican institutions for the moral education of the people became apparent in practice, his enthusiasm was greeted with excited approval by more moderate, liberal-minded theorists. Rœderer, for example, friend and intellectual associate of both Condorcet and the Abbé Sieyès, commented that here at last was someone who had outlined to the Convention in April 1793 the need to insert something between precepts and powers in the forthcoming constitution.[30] Between the Declaration of Rights and the constitution, between principles and laws, there was a need for institutions that would shape the wills and habits of citizens in accordance with the general interest. Saint-Just, as this intelligent and politically alert contemporary interpreter understood him, hoped to merge the general interest and individual habits, offsetting the twin dangers of oppression by public power, and abandonment to the frivolity and self-centeredness of private interest.

Here Saint-Just was at a turning point. He argued that government should be less authoritarian than a principle or spring of social harmony. But he also invoked Rousseau to argue that the Legislator should mold man as he needed him to be. And during the summer of 1793 he claimed that if the people who had been given a *patrie* were not happy, there must be something wrong with them.[31] There was a surprising and shockingly short step between the view that social harmony could not exist independently of political institutions, and the view that individuals should be altered to fit with the institutions they had acquired. By February 1794 Saint-Just was claiming: "Il s'est fait une révolution dans le gouvernement; elle n'a point pénétré l'état civil." But the penetration of government into society in any directly authoritarian sense was the precise inverse of the schemes for enhancing cooperation and spontaneous social harmony that Condorcet, Brissot, Rœderer, and many others had tried to develop before the outbreak of the Terror.

Conclusion

During the French Revolution, the problem of reconciling individual rights with communal (or simply social) life reached far wider than the Jacobins. It was one form of a problem that lies at the heart of all societies, revolutionary or otherwise: when are individuals to be coerced, how far is this justified, and how far can it be avoided? In this context, Robespierre, perhaps the most famous of all the Jacobins, is also the least instructive. As an ardent individualist who believed that the people was good in itself, and that virtue, or *patrie*, could be equated with popular sovereignty, Robespierre managed to ignore the question of coercion during the early years of the French Revolution, except when he passionately objected to the ways in which it was exercised. His abrupt reversal on this point when he assumed governing power was less a matter of hypocrisy than a violently exaggerated response to a rude awakening. He postponed non-coercive government until the republic was at last secure, arguing that "La protection sociale n'est due qu'aux citoyens paisibles; il n'y a de citoyens dans la République que les républicains."

Condorcet, Brissot, Rœderer, and others had been facing the problem of coercion more steadily, with greater clarity of mind, and for much longer. Condorcet hoped that public education would extend the competence of the citizens so that they were less likely to pose a threat to liberty in and of themselves, and more capable of ensuring that their governors did not do so either. Brissot was less optimistic about extending the competence of the people, and instead proposed tutors of the people to mediate between them and their governors. Virtue was required to bridge the gap between the individual and social cohesion. Rœderer set out to judge the nature and extent of spontaneously occurring social cohesion inside modern commercial society, claiming that until this was known it would be impossible to judge how strong a government was required to maintain social order. He argued that in any society the legislative body needed to understand how the energy and intensity of moral passions could be controlled or influenced. It was not, he insisted, his intention to suggest that the state should treat its citizens as a doctor treats his patients: as subjects in need of a cure. But as Saint-Just was soon to demonstrate, this was a very fine line to tread. Designing institutions to foster social cooperation was one way to avoid direct coercion of individuals by their governors. But these same institutions were conduits for coercion in and of themselves.[32]

The dividing line between these revolutionaries did not lie in the degree of their esteem for institutions with the capacity for molding individuals and adapting them for social life. The real dividing lines lay elsewhere: in complex judgments about the timing and extent of the sacrifices that it is appropriate or practical for a society to demand from its citizens; and in ever-more intricate accounts of the relationship between individual, economic, and political freedom. If virtue is understood in these terms, there is a case for returning to Wollstonecraft's claim that "the virtues of a nation bear an exact proportion to their scientific improvements." It would then, however, be appropriate, if somewhat self-aggrandizing, to refine the quotation to read: "the virtues of a nation bear an exact proportion to their improvements in political science." And it would be essential to add that improvement in political science in practice is likely to depend largely on the stability of the institutional setting in which the citizens of a particular nation find themselves. That is, in the extent to which history has already provided the conditions of relative calm in which it is possible to learn cumulatively. Whatever passions are to be engaged or relied on, it is never safe to trust fear (or terror) alone.

Notes

1.   Wollstonecraft and Godwin, 1987, Letter 19.
2.   For a detailed account of the development in Wollstonecraft's view of and reaction to the French Revolution, see Todd, 2000.

3.   Higgonet, 1998.
4.   Higgonet, 1998, p. 1.
5.   Higgonet, 1998, p. 1.
6.   See Fontana (ed.), 1994.
7.   See Robbins, 1959; Pocock, 1985; Hont and Ignatieff (eds.), 1983.
8.   Montesquieu, [1748], 1950–61; Mably, 1789; Rousseau, 1962.
9.   Van Kley, 1996, pp. 296–297.
10.   Ibid., pp. 218–219.
11.   The political importance of the concepts of virtue and its inverse, egoism, has been emphasized by historians of the French Revolution since Guizot. It was of particular importance to the Marxist interpretations of the Revolution. See Soboul, 1964. See also Jaurès, 1968; Mathiez, 1927; and Lefebvre, 1964.
12.   See also Jaume, 1989. Compare the revolutionary vigilance of the sans-culottes, described in Soboul, 1964.
13.   Montesquieu, 1950–61. For secondary sources on Montesquieu, see particularly, Keohane, 1980; and Ellis, pp. 61–81.
14.   Condorcet was permanent secretary of the Academy of Sciences on the eve of the Revolution in 1789. He played an active part in the politics of the early revolutionary years, altering and refining his political thinking as a result. He died in gaol during the Terror in 1794. See especially Baker, 1975. Brissot was a prominent revolutionary journalist and publisher, and a leader of the so-called Girondin faction that opposed Robespierre's ascendancy at the Jacobin Club after 1791. He was guillotined during the Terror. See Kates, 1985; and Brissot, 1911. Robespierre's arrest and execution in 1794 marks the official, if not the actual, end of the Terror. See especially Haydon and Doyle (eds.), 1999; and Thompson, 1939; and Robespierre, 1910–67. Saint-Just accompanied Robespierre to the guillotine, still championing the need for republican institutions—the means of fostering patriotic virtue that meant so much to him. See Hampson, 1991; and Saint-Just, 1984.
15.   Montesquieu, 1950–61, part 1, book 1.
16.   Ibid., part 1, book 1, chapter 5.
17.   Necker, 1792.
18.   Gueniffey, 1994, pp. 86–106, p. 98. Caritat, marquis de Condorcet, [1786] 1847–49, vol. 5, pp. 209–10.
19.   Gueniffey, 1994, p. 100; Condorcet, 1847–49, vol. 9, pp. 378–83.
20.   Baker, 1975, pp. 316–20.
21.   Archives Parlementaires de 1787 à 1860, Debats Législatifs et Politiques des chambres Françaises, sous la direction de Mavidal et de Laurent, Première Serie, 1787–1799, 82 vols. Paris: Librarie administrative de Paul Dupont, 1885, [AP hereafter], 21 décembre 1792.
22.   Gueniffey, 1994, p. 96; Le Patriote françois, Journal Libre et impartial, Paris (6 May 1789–31 Dec. 1792, no. 696–97, 17 March, 1791.)
23.   See Œuvres de Sieyès, 1989.
24.   Gueniffey, 1994, p. 101.
25.   Cobban, 1971, pp. 137–59.
26.   Ibid., pp. 159–92.
27.   Ibid., p. 170.
28.   Hampson, 1988, pp. 125–39.
29.   Hampson, 1988 and 1991.
30.   Journal de Paris, Paris (1777–1827), 25 April 1793. On Rœderer see especially Forsyth, 1989.
31.   Hampson, 1988.
32.   Foucault, 1975; Foucault, 2001.

8

Volunteering as Virtue

Bryan S. Turner

Introduction: Paradox of Volunteering as a Virtue

While the notion of voluntary action has been of interest to philosophers, my approach to the issue of volunteering is primarily sociological. I am interested in voluntary acts, but more particularly with the institutionalization of volunteering, and the place of volunteering within a modern economy. This discussion revolves around the tensions between a virtuous act (volunteering), an institution (voluntary association), and the market. The sociological question is whether volunteering has a place in societies where voluntary work and voluntary associations have either been absorbed by the welfare state, or where voluntary services increasingly come under the control of professional managers who work for a salary. Several questions look prima facie interesting: do voluntary associations have a place in a socialist society, and can volunteering be a virtue under socialism? Can volunteering survive commercialization in a capitalist economy?

In order to answer these questions, my argument is primarily concerned with volunteering for social purposes, and thus with the contributions of volunteering and voluntarism to the making and maintenance of welfare services. The argument is consequently less concerned with volunteering in cultural institutions, with voluntary sports organizations, or with voluntary contributions to religious organizations. In part, this focus on volunteering for social purposes serves to identify the paradoxical relationships between personal independence and autonomy on the one hand, and the collectivist principles of the welfare state on the other. Neo-liberal and conservative critics of traditional welfare states have criticized the welfare state bureaucracy, because it created individual dependency.

In Britain, the postwar welfare state, it is alleged, created personal dependency from the cradle to the grave. The Thatcherite revolution was intended to roll back the state and to force people to take more direct responsibility for education, welfare, and health provision through private means. This strategy also required a larger role for voluntary associations in the welfare sector. Third-Way welfare policies of New Labour in Britain and elsewhere have also promoted the idea of voluntary associations and volunteering as alternatives to welfare dependency, because they are seen to be more compatible with individual responsibility and autonomy. Thus, in many advanced capitalist societies, volunteering and voluntary associations are not only approved and promoted, they are regarded as an essential, if threatened, feature of modern society, as they contribute directly to social capital. President George W. Bush has made "faith-based associations" an important part of his social policies, and in British politics Blair and Brown have claimed that voluntary activities and associations are a foundation of their view of society. Advocates of Third-Way strategies are generally enthusiastic about voluntary associations since they are thought to be important to refurbish trust and build up social capital.[1]

This observation suggests a simple model in which social democratic welfare policies and the growth of state welfare should diminish the importance of voluntary contributions, whereas neo-liberal deregulation of welfare provision should restore the importance of voluntary associations and bring about a revaluation of the virtue of volunteering. In order to examine this causal connection, it is instructive to compare the United States, Britain, and Sweden. One theme of this comparative sketch is that traditional forms of voluntary activity have experienced a process of professionalization and voluntary associations are driven by the logic of resource maximization in which the differentiation between *profit*, *not-for-profit*, and *nonprofit* is obscured. As a result, voluntary workers have been transformed into professional salaried employees in large, professional nonprofit organizations or community enterprises. In terms of Max Weber's economic sociology, this development is an example of the rationalization of volunteerism in a developed capitalist economy.

This historical and sociological interpretation of volunteering in relation to the growth of state structures is a useful point of departure, but it is clearly too simple to be satisfactory. There is at least one crucial addition to this argument, namely the role of religion and religious institutions in supporting the idea of voluntarism. Before the rise of the modern state, religious foundations were major conduits of voluntary (and more generally charitable) acts. For example, the hospital grew out of religious charities that provided hospitality on a voluntary basis to travelers involved in religious pilgrimages. In traditional Christian societies, volunteering and voluntary work for the needy were regarded as religious activities. For example, Christ's washing the feet of his followers has been taken as the ultimate religious authority for voluntary services as a religious virtue. It is ironic, however, that the modern meaning of 'volunteer' owes as much to voluntary military service for the state as it does to acts of charity towards the poor. Any account of voluntary activities as virtuous would need to examine these two dimensions: military service and charitable acts.

In many cultures, volunteering was historically interpreted as virtuous, but in modern societies there is also the notion that it has questionable consequences for the recipient (in promoting dependency) and the giver (by engendering false or overweening superiority). The underlying contemporary objection against regarding volunteering (or charity more generally) as virtuous is that it must presuppose the existence of a social hierarchy of power and need. In a society with a definite and formal system of status honor, voluntary work towards the poor reaffirms the moral worth of the provider and the religious value of poverty. There is a functional relationship of exchange where those at the top of a status hierarchy receive a spiritual reward, implicit or explicit, for their voluntary acts. In a modern society that has fully absorbed Nietzsche's combined criticisms of Christian morality and British utilitarianism, we are more likely to regard volunteering as a disguised act of symbolic violence against the poor and needy. What Nietzsche called 'the mask of philanthropy' is a form of institutionalized humiliation that reproduces a system of inequality.[2] A skeptic steeped in Nietzsche's deconstruction of moral masks might ask, when confronted by an earnest volunteer: What's in it for you?

While in many modern economies voluntary associations are seen to be an essential element of social capital, the individual act of volunteering is often regarded with some suspicion. Volunteering, in a society that places a high value on efficiency and professionalism, may also be associated with amateurism. In liberal societies that promote professionalism, volunteering is associated with the patronizing and hypocritical attitudes of the Victorian period. Volunteering finally is often ascribed negative gender attributes, because women have typically contributed more to voluntary associations than have men. Voluntary work has been historically the unpaid work of women. In Britain, sixty-five percent of voluntary sector employees are female, whereas women represent only thirty-nine percent of private sector employees. Is volunteering, then, a virtue in a secular society with a considerable amount of state provision, where managerial philosophies expect voluntary work in nonprofit organizations to be professional? Do Third-Way welfare strategies in fact spell the end of volunteering?

A Preliminary Outline of the Social Structure of Volunteering

There are two somewhat distinct meanings for volunteering and volunteers in the English language. *The Oxford English Dictionary* notes that the term "volunteer" dates from the seventeenth century and refers to an auxiliary military force of voluntary recruits (1642). "Volunteering" occurs in 1691 to refer to voluntary military service. By the middle of the eighteenth century, it included any form of service undertaken on a voluntary basis. By 1834, "volunteer" designated a person who held that the Church and educational institutions should be maintained by voluntary subscriptions rather than by the state, and hence "voluntaryism" (1835) is the principle that religious and educational institutions should be supported by voluntary contributions and not by the state. The tradition of military volunteering is well established in Britain as a means of defense against invasion. The threat of French invasion or Jacobite disturbance saw the recruitment of volunteers in 1715 and 1745, in 1779 during the American War of Independence, and during the Napoleonic wars. In Ireland, the volunteer movement also emerged in response to the threat of invasion and before the peace of 1783 was able to exert pressure on the British government over parliamentary reform and Catholic representation. In America, the growth of voluntary associations was directly related to the civil war. Between the 1820s and 1850s, there was a rapid expansion of nationwide membership associations, such as religious and moral reform groups. From the 1860s to the 1920s, there was an equally strong growth of such associations, especially veterans and patriotic societies.[3]

This brief overview of the history of volunteering and volunteers indicates sociologically that volunteering, becoming a significant and socially recognized activity in British society between 1620 and 1870, can only make sense against the presence of a contrast case: the cash nexus and a capitalist labor market. Voluntary labor is virtuous in a society where the payment and exploitation of labor has become the dominant mode of social exchange. With the rise of a capitalist society, the contributions of labor to production become precisely measured by units of time and rewarded exclusively by wages. Voluntary gifts of money (philanthropy), investments (charities), and labor (volunteering) are virtuous because they are publicly recognized as contributions to the needy, marginal, and the poor that fall outside the cash nexus. Unpaid altruistic volunteering appears virtuous precisely because the measurement and payment of labor time is the basis of economic activity.

Volunteering changes when the dominance of the cash nexus is modified. In a social democratic environment, volunteering is partly or wholly replaced by the state. Individual citizens involuntarily contribute to the poor through compulsory taxation or through involvement in community activities that are supported by or incorporated within the state. In advanced capitalism, volunteering declines, because the voluntary sector is partially included in the market (through commercialization or through the creation of community enterprise strategies). The management of the sector is professional, and is recruited on the basis of competitive salaries. From the nineteenth century, these voluntary acts and organizations have been gradually institutionalized into a system of welfare that is very dependent on the state as a source of funding. In 1995, British voluntary associations received forty-six percent of its income from the government and only nine percent from private donations.

From the point of view of political economy, volunteering requires a class system or a definite hierarchy of status groups in which the voluntary contribution of unpaid labor to an underclass has moral worth. Because voluntary acts require an exchange relationship of dependency and inequality, volunteering has offended socialist sensibilities about equality of condition. Classical economics paid little attention to voluntary labor, because it was not easily accommodated to the basic division between productive and unproductive labor. In any case, political economy was more likely to follow Mandeville's *The Fable of the Bees,* in which private vices (greed) produce public benefits (economic growth). Mandeville's argument was an attack on Shaftesbury's belief that human beings were naturally altruistic and that benevolence produced a public benefit, and promoted the optimistic view that the hidden hand of history would bring about a reconciliation of the conflicts of self-interest. British moral philosophy after Mandeville did not produce an entirely convincing argument about benevolence, but philosophers continued to assume the moral priority of benevolent over self-interested actions.

Sociologists have found more inspiration in Thorstein Veblen's class analysis than in classical economics as a perspective on voluntary activity. In *The Theory of the Leisure Class*, voluntary labor was considered economically unproductive because it does not by definition receive a wage, but it had enormous social benefit in confirming the social status of voluntary work.[4] From the point of view of Veblen's cultural theory, upper-class men could enjoy vicariously the cultural capital that emerged from the voluntary work of their leisurely wives. A leisure class, based on the "non-productive consumption time" makes voluntary work acceptable to a leisure class that wants to display its "conspicuous leisure" through such charitable activities.[5] Volunteering has been historically dominated by women from the middle and upper classes who had the time and resources to support charities and voluntary associations. As women have entered the formal labor force in the postwar period, voluntary associations have not been able to access this pool of voluntary labor easily, and they have become more dependent on paid labor and professional management. The cultural capital of voluntary work is still expected from that ultimate remnant of the leisure class—the Royal family. We can now formulate a preliminary theory of voluntary work. In a society that is dominated by capitalist production, and where the majority of the population sells its labor power in return for wages in order to satisfy its basic needs, voluntary work involves an expenditure of labor that satisfies the need for cultural capital and hence for social distinction.[6] It is virtuous precisely because it does not fall under the logic of self-interest in that it does not satisfy mundane, indeed profane, needs.

It could be claimed that this argument from a political economy of philanthropy does not provide a satisfactory account of why people volunteer. There are a number of standard explanations about the rise and functions of voluntary organizations. These organizations can arise because of the failure of state provision or because people trust the voluntary sector more than government agencies.[7] The voluntary welfare sector, especially in the health field, has expanded, precisely as the state in Britain, Australia, and New Zealand has been rolled back.[8] But why do individuals behave philanthropically and why do they volunteer? In a materialist culture, caring and giving are, or can be, expressions of spirituality as an antidote to the material values of capitalism,[9] but the dominant explanations for philanthropy are, as I have noted, predominantly neo-classical explanations of rational action. People give money or time, because they calculate a personal benefit: social recognition, spiritual rewards, or personal satisfaction.

From a sociological point of view, however, it is important to examine volunteering as a social relationship. It is difficult to see how welfare volunteering (as opposed to military volunteering) could exist without an audience or client group, without a class of people who are unable to meet their own needs. Furthermore, these audiences of the needy have to be strangers. We do not define the care of children by their mothers as "voluntary work"; parenthood is not volunteering, because it is regarded as a familial duty or obligation.[10] Voluntary work is freely undertaken in the service of needy strangers. It is virtuous because the recipient can have no expectation of provision where there is no obligation to serve. It is this neutrality of the social relationship that provides evidence that the voluntary work is disinterested.

In order for volunteering to exist, there must be a social structure of systematic inequality. Social stratification can involve both class and status inequalities of material and symbolic inequality. Weber's account of mendicity among Theravada Buddhist monks is a good sociological example. Weber famously described Buddhism as "a specifically unpolitical and anti-political status religion, more precisely a religious 'technology' of wandering and of intellectually schooled monks."[11] The monks demonstrate their spiritual status by renouncing worldly wealth and office, and become dependent on gifts, especially rice, from the laity that remains locked within the world. Such a system involves a circulation of benefits in which monks exchange charisma in the form of blessings that confer health for rice that keeps the monks alive. Weber calls this system a structure of virtuoso-mass religion. The virtuosity of monastic practice requires a transfer of charisma in a society that is deeply divided by status. This form of religious virtue is not confined to Buddhism; it occurs whenever charismatic healing powers are sought by a lay audience.[12]

A moral philosopher, contemplating the ascetic traditions of Christianity, might object to these arguments on the ground that the sociological and neo-classical explanations of volunteering involve a crude psychological reductionism and therefore miss the point. A voluntary act can be virtuous only if it is disinterested; it has no purpose, no moral status, and no meaning beyond itself. Voluntary activity can bring no merit and no reward to the individual who provides it. It must be a pure expression of care. One might take the argument even further: the voluntary nature of the act cannot be praised without bringing into question the moral status of the act. Where possible, a voluntary act of charity should remain anonymous, because it is only where the provider remains anonymous to the recipient that the virtue of the act can be maintained.

One reply to these objections is that in fact the Christian tradition has itself been divided over the nature of moral virtue. It is conventional to distinguish between eudaimonism and deontology.[13] The first considers happiness as a valid reason for undertaking charitable activities in the love of our neighbors. Virtues are rewarded in heaven, and therefore volunteering increases my happiness. In this sense, explanations that appeal to eudaimonist principles are arguments of (psychological) utility. Deontological arguments tend to suggest that virtue is desirable for its own sake and that volunteering is good because it conforms to moral laws. Augustine's theory of virtue was both eudaimonian and deontological,[14] because it explains the love of neighbors as both for the sake of God, and for its own sake. Christian explanations of virtue have subsequently been divided in their emphasis on utility or deontology. There is also the troublesome issue of free will. The virtue of voluntary work requires that it is an expression of care and assumes the free will of the agent. Christian theories of virtue, and Augustinian theory in particular, confront a difficulty in that the charity and virtue of the Christian are in fact manifestations of divine love. An Augustinian saint cannot choose virtue anymore than he or she could choose sin, because their good works are causally determined by grace.[15] However, if grace is irresistible for saints, can it be virtuous?

Tocqueville, Volunteering, and Moral Citizenship in America

Volunteering and voluntary associations have been central to American liberal theory and fundamental to American democracy. America provides, in the case of volunteering, the major example of liberal virtues. Liberalism emphasizes personal autonomy, moral responsibility, and activism. Liberty of association is a necessary condition of liberal virtue. We may expect "liberal citizens to be prepared to combine in voluntary associations for common ends both altruistic and otherwise. Autonomous liberal subjects will prize not isolated activity but the liberty to choose how to be associated, with whom, in what manner, and for what purposes."[16] It is thus fundamentally incorrect to assume that liberal individualism values isolated forms of self-gratification, and, as Macedo points out, liberalism cherishes the clubs and associations that flourish in a free society.

The normative sources of this liberal vision are Alexis de Tocqueville's political analyses of 1835 and 1840 on democracy in America.[17] Voluntary associations were the social core of American civil society, and an essential element in sustaining individual freedoms and conscience against the impact of the egalitarian principle of a mass democracy. By comparison with France, Tocqueville observed how American settlers routinely cooperated with each other to satisfy a social need such as the building of a school or church. Whereas in France the government would undertake such activities, or in England an aristocrat would undertake such tasks, in America it was an association. Voluntary organizations were a check on the state and also helped to create a society that was diverse and pluralistic. Such associations were in part an outgrowth of colonial experience, where the settlement and pacification of the frontier required collective involvement.

The formation of a militia was an important illustration of voluntary activity, but it was also an important platform of participatory citizenship. The regulations for the control of the militia, such as the Militia Act of 1792, drew a clear racial division in calling for the recruitment of able-bodied white men. If the motives for welfare voluntarism appear to be ambiguous, the motivations of military volunteers were explicitly utilitarian. The militia existed to protect property and offer defense. In her recent work, Theda Skocpol has drawn attention to the impact of the Civil War and the Union victory on the great expansion of civil associations: these associations were important in rebuilding American society and "after the war, Americans were looking to put their lives back together again through community building activities."[18]

Contemporary studies of American politics and culture continue to evoke this Tocquevillian legacy. In their influential study of associationalism, Joshua Cohen and Joel Rogers have brought together the Tocquevillian legacy by arguing that voluntary associations have four democracy-enhancing functions:[19] (1) They provide information to policymakers. (2) They redress political inequalities that exist when politics is materially based. (3) They can act as schools of democracy and (4) they provide alternative governance to markets and public hierarchies, which permits society to realize the important benefits of cooperation among citizens. Nonprofit organizations are a crucial condition of political participation: they are more efficient than government provision and can be more sensitive and responsive to the needs of client groups; they are crucial for the reproduction of social capital that underpins effective democratic political systems and strong economies; and they provide for a strong civil society that outweighs the tendencies towards domination of the state and market forces.

This Tocquevillian legacy has been the inspiration behind Robert Bellah's *The Habits of the Heart*, which documented the decline of the public arena in American life and showed how political values and interests were channeled through local community groups and voluntary associations.[20] Among contemporary American sociologists, there has been a consensus about the positive effects of voluntary associations, especially in Robert Wuthnow's *Acts of Compassion* and *Poor Richard's Principle*, where voluntarism is an essential underpinning of caring for others.[21] Thus, the legacy of research on voluntary associations has been gradually incorporated into communitarianism and the decline of such organizations in America is taken as a forceful measure of the erosion of citizenship.[22]

The British Welfare State and Swedish Social Democracy

Modern society is no longer constituted of a dense network of associations, clubs, fraternities, chapels, working men's societies, and communal associations. The late twentieth century has been marked by a major decline in all forms of social participation, at least partly as a consequence of the impact of television on leisure activities. Religious membership, confirmations, baptism, and marriages in the mainstream Christian churches have declined considerably since 1970, although there has been an increase in evangelical sects and in non-Christian religions. Membership in political parties and newspaper readership have also declined in Britain. Whereas seventy-six percent of men and sixty-eight percent of women claimed to read a newspaper in 1981, newspaper readership had declined to sixty and fifty-one percent by 1998–9. These changes raise questions about the possibilities of participation in contemporary society, and specifically about the level of third-sector institutions, such as voluntary associations, in providing opportunities for social service and participation. It is generally recognized that individual giving to charities and voluntary associations has steadily declined in the postwar period.

The conventional assumption is that participation in the voluntary sector has, like other forms of social involvement, declined through the twentieth century, but this pessimistic interpretation appears to underestimate the importance of charities, voluntary associations, and philanthropy. For example, about one quarter of the British population claim to have participated in a voluntary association in the previous year, and of these about half spent twenty days or more in voluntary activities. Around seventy percent of the British population donates to charities and seventy percent volunteer every year. In 1999, the gross income of charities was around £15 billion and the average per capita donations per annum amounts to £100.[23] Voluntary organizations employ about two percent of the work force. While the membership of some associations has fallen, other associations have grown rapidly. For example, although the membership of the Mothers' Union fell from 308,000 to 177,000 between 1971 and 1990, membership of the National Trust increased from 278,000 to just over two million in the same period.[24] Membership of voluntary associations increased from 0.73 memberships per capita in 1959 to 1.12 memberships in 1990. Individual involvement in voluntary associations, clubs, and leisure groups is probably more robust than the Putnam thesis about the decline of social capital would suggest.

If, however, we simply count the number of voluntary associations and chart their growth, it is evident that voluntary associations, especially in the welfare sector, have expanded significantly in the last twenty years, and in part this growth can be attributed to the decline of state activity in welfare. The Johns Hopkins Comparative Nonprofit Sector Project discovered that, in the seven countries studied, one in every twenty jobs, and one in every eight service jobs are accounted for by the voluntary sector. The rolling back of the state appears to have created a social vacuum in which the third sector has expanded to satisfy communal needs.

Voluntary associations in welfare provision have adopted innovative market approaches to welfare, often based on partnerships between the market, the state, and the voluntary sector. For many critics of market-driven social policies (such as Thatcherism, Reagonomics, and managerialism), the reduction of state support for welfare was automatically taken to be a measure of the decline of social citizenship, but this argument ignores the fact that many features of the postwar welfare state were bureaucratic, paternalistic, and exclusionary. For critics of socialist social policy, such as F.A. Hayek and Enoch Powell, state bureaucracies were thought to undermine individual freedoms and create psychological dependency. While we should not exaggerate the degree of postwar political consensus as to the role of the state in welfare provision in the immediate aftermath of the Second World War, criticism of the legacy of Butskellism and "bureaucratic collectivism" became increasingly strident in the 1970s. The welfare bureaucracy was an obvious target of right wing criticism in the Thatcher years, but left wing and liberal critics of bureaucratic welfare were equally antagonistic towards invasive welfare processes, especially means-tested support. In the period leading up to the election of Mrs. Thatcher's Conservative government in 1979, there was a paradoxical agreement between the left and right wings of British politics that the welfare state was in crisis. The solution adopted by the Thatcher and Major governments (1979–97) was to reduce public expenditure on welfare, privatize national industries, and cut personal taxation. The new consensus of the Blair government places greater emphasis on Third-Way strategies, part of which involves a quest either for partnerships between government and third-sector organizations or direct encouragement of the voluntary sector to provide local and community-based services. Given dissatisfaction with the negative consequences of the market as a solution to social and political questions, reliance on the voluntary sector is compatible with the search for active citizenship, associative democracy, and subsidiarity in service provision. The underlying assumption is that a vibrant democracy is unlikely to flourish without authentic community, but whether or not voluntary associations can provide an effective welfare service is possibly less important than whether they can provide an experience of community involvement that in turn can be a schooling in democracy.

In Britain, the associative democracy debate had its intellectual and political location in the problems presented by an "electoral dictatorship" that emerged during the Thatcher years (1979–90), when there appeared to be no effective political opposition to the social and economic policies of a determined leader with a precarious majority in the Commons. Associative democracy was conceptualized as a political response to an erosion of the institutional framework of strong opposition, and it was elaborated to include stronger notions of participation. Modern theories of associational democracy argue that voluntary associations provide local opportunities for representation, offer opportunities for active citizenship by encouraging participation, and thus contribute to civic culture, contain the spread of bureaucracy in political organizations, and foster pluralism and diversity. In *Associative Democracy*, Paul Q. Hirst argues that voluntary associations have the potential to be the principal organizing force in society providing public welfare and the primary means of democratic governance.[25] Indeed, if government really is part of the problem, then Hirst's proposal should be all the more attractive, since its primary aim is to reduce the scale and scope of the affairs administered by the state. Subsidiarity would be achieved through a process of devolution of state functions, authority, and funding to a network of voluntary associations. Such a system would support a process where citizen choice is combined with public welfare and, because voluntary associations have the capacity for a high level of communicative democracy, this devolved political structure would allow for widespread consultation, cooperation, and collaboration. Voluntary associations are characterized by organizational autonomy from the state and, where their internal organizational structures support client involvement, they are better suited to promoting welfare that is targeted to local communities than are state bureaucracies.

We must in any case start with a definition. Voluntary associations can be said to have five characteristics: they are organized, private, nonprofit-distributing, self-governing, and voluntary.[26] The sociological debate around voluntary associations has been concerned with exploring their autonomy and independence in relation to both the state and the market. In the British context, the connection between government and voluntary association has been historically very close. On the one hand, the creation of the National Health Service and welfare state transferred existing services from the private to the public sector; on the other hand, the rolling back of the state has simply reversed that process. They are defined as private, because they exist between government and market; they are also civil society organizations. There are some difficulties with this location of the voluntary sector, because in practice their connections with government are very strong. There are, for example, a variety of funding arrangements in Great Britain, which indicate the close relationships between government and voluntary organizations— including direct financial support and tax concessions.[27] The national lottery also channels funding into the voluntary sector under the regulation of the government. The development of an enterprise culture has promoted the idea of social investments and the growth of enterprise communities that ideologically tend to be antagonistic towards voluntary organizations.

There is also considerable ambiguity in the relationship of voluntary associations to the economy. Traditionally, voluntary associations were not expected to function like business organizations and their funding came from philanthropic donations, bequests, and other gifts. Although voluntary associations are still either nonprofit or not-for-profit organizations, they are increasingly under economic pressure to marketize and commodify their services. In order to generate funding, they have to compete for government grants, and so there is pressure for these associations to become more professional. They need to hire staff who are highly qualified, not only to run large and complex organizations, but who are knowledgeable about government strategy, costing, and managing projects. These managerial developments increasingly produce a division between the board of managers and the rank and file. There appears to be an inherent tension in how voluntary associations are organized, because the growth of professional values may conflict with traditional notions of philanthropy. The rise of generic management illustrates a common professionalization of the sector. The functions and composition of the boards of voluntary associations have been critically discussed in the social policy literature because they are sensitive sites of public debate and concern. It is also assumed that voluntary associations will be self-governing. The pressure to professionalize in order to increase financial resources also creates new problems about responsibility, access, and participation. These management issues are important, given the fact that the voluntary sector is regarded as the spearhead of grassroots democratization. If voluntary associations become large and bureaucratic, they cannot remain sensitive to local or client interests, and they reproduce the worst features of traditional, top-down welfare bureaucracies.

The voluntary sector is now under the same financial and management pressures that shape capitalist corporations, and therefore voluntary associations are driven by a logic of resource maximization and enhancement;[28] they are forced to employ and promote managerial rationality (and thus to recruit from a pool of generic management); they are compelled to professionalize their processes of recruitment and training; and they are dependent on rational and professional systems of fundraising. In Britain, they are very dependent on their ability to tender successfully for government grants. There is therefore some force to the conventional criticisms of the voluntary sector: it cannot provide a universalistic service, it does not have clear performance criteria, it is not rigorously accountable, and it may not be cost effective. A diverse and successful voluntary sector cannot address the social divisions and inequality of a capitalist system.[29] Worse still, voluntary associations may often function more like social clubs than service agencies, and they may form a social hierarchy of agencies that is a mirror image of the status hierarchy of society as a whole. Some charities and voluntary associations simply serve the "expressive needs" of the middle classes and provide social outlets for unpaid work from the middle classes (Pearce, 1993). In both America and Britain, there developed a critical research literature in the 1970s that suggested that voluntary associations functioned to restrain wage increases in social services as a result of competition between paid and unpaid workers.[30] The economic and legal framework within which the voluntary sector operates in the United Kingdom is not conducive to sustaining its more idealistic or Tocquevillian objectives of democratization.[31]

Sweden can be taken to be a classic illustration of social democracy with an extensive welfare sector that is dominated by the state. There has been a tendency among some Swedish social scientists to argue that in fact Sweden does not have a voluntary sector. The absence of voluntary work would be consistent with my (paradoxi-

cal) argument that voluntary activity is significant in (early) capitalism alongside a laboring class, but the voluntary principle declines
with a process of professionalization. In so far as Swedish society
has modified the wage relationship by a welfare state, it should not
have a significant tradition of voluntary associations. There is therefore a plausible argument that the third sector is underdeveloped in
Sweden, as since the nineteenth century the state has played an important part in building and directing welfare services.[32]

This interpretation of Sweden has been challenged.[33] Research
data show that the Swedish nonprofit sector makes an important
contribution to culture and recreation (twenty-two percent of the
sector expenditures), but the voluntary nonprofit sector makes, by
comparison with Britain, a relatively small contribution to health
care and social services.[34] Research in medical sociology has suggested that, in general, membership of civil associations is strong in
the Nordic countries and that, as a measure of social cohesion, this
social involvement contributes to the low mortality rates in these
societies (Carlson, 1998).

Sweden is a primary illustration of a social democratic welfare
system in which private charity and volunteering have little place,
because state intervention has prevented the commodification of
social rights and attempted to set universal standards. As we have
already noted, voluntary principles in a liberal regime will not universally address the problem of social inequality. In *The Three Worlds
of Welfare Capitalism*, Esping-Andersen analyzes Sweden as a principal illustration of the de-commodification of welfare services, where
the middle classes are successfully incorporated into a welfare regime that espouses universal social rights.[35] It is significant that his
treatment of the social democratic regime has no reference to voluntary principles in relation to the building of the Swedish welfare state.
By contrast, a voluntary element was indispensable to the Beverage
approach to welfare. The social democratic principle appears to have
survived in Sweden despite significant economic pressures to modify
its welfare regime. While in Sweden there is an important element of
community participation in welfare provision, the liberal model of
voluntarism has not had much impact.

Conclusion: Weber and Rationalization

This discussion of voluntary work and the modern economy can
be seen as a contribution to Weber's meta-theoretical perspective on

the rationalization of culture. The gradual expansion of a modern labor market, the institutionalization of welfare functions through the state and the private sectors, the professionalization of volunteering, and managerial hostility to amateurism have brought about the end of what we may call "pure volunteering." The social death of "pure volunteering" has meant that voluntary work for social purposes can no longer function as a virtue. To my knowledge, Weber did not write on the sociology of voluntary labor, but he did produce an interesting commentary on the decline of charity that provides a template for how one might develop a more complete sociology of volunteering. Weber provides a sketch in *Economy and Society* of how almsgiving and charity are generalizations of the assumption that a co-religionist has a right of assistance.[36]

The religious injunction to love one's neighbor raises the obvious question: Who is my neighbor? Weber presented a sociological comment on the roots of religious cosmopolitanism by claiming that the development of the idea of universal love is only possible "after political and ethnic communities have become considerably intermingled and after the gods have been liberated from connection with political organizations to become universal powers."[37] With economic differentiation, customs of neighborly assistance are transformed into customs between social strata, and the contributions of the wealthy through almsgiving and charity receive the praises of the poor who cannot reciprocate in this world. The giving of alms thus becomes a primary component of every ethical religion. In Christianity, the responsibility of the wealthy to support the poor in order to support their own salvation was sufficiently powerful for the poor to become a separate status group. Charitable assistance to the faithful in sectarian religious groups became a welfare insurance, but as these congregational religions declined, charity lost its significance.

Charity developed as a personal relationship of mutual benefit between the rich and the poor. Almsgiving and charity are reflections of a more general condemnation of usury as unregulated profit seeking that is damaging to the community. One might say, following Augustine: No *caritas* without *cupiditas*. One consequence of the growth of capitalist relationships is the depersonalization of social relationships as a development of the rationalization of life. Weber writes:

Rational economic association always brings about depersonalization, and it is impossible to control a universe of instrumentally rational activities by charitable appeals to particular individuals. The functional world of capitalism certainly offers no support for any such charitable orientation.[38]

There were important variations within Christianity in relationship to the growth of capitalism. In particular, Calvinism destroyed traditional, unsystematic patterns of charity. Whereas random or contingent almsgiving had always been regarded as a good work, Calvinism institutionalized almsgiving to the poor and widows in order to undermine the role of begging as a special type of occupation. Calvinism precluded any benevolent attitude towards beggars and reminded its congregations that charity did not exist to reward the idle. Weber concluded this commentary on the history of almsgiving with the Puritans from whom

[c]are of the poor was oriented to the goal of discouraging the slothful.... Charity itself became an 'enterprise' and its religious significance was therefore eliminated or even transformed into the opposite significance. This was the situation in consistent ascetic and rationalized religions.[39]

There is a clear paradox here that is fateful. Volunteering cannot come fully into existence without a capitalist labor market, because its meaning is parasitic upon, or at least contrasted with, the idea of self-interest and paid work. Ideas about charity and philanthropy have their origins in the Christian idea of brotherly love and were articulated in Augustine's theory of the virtues. These values formed the basis of the idea of a brotherly community that was contrasted with usury and greed. But pure volunteering is paradoxically inseparable from a money economy, a class system, and wage labor. In contemporary Britain, voluntary associations are professional organizations that deliver welfare with the broad support of the state, because a welfare system that combines state and voluntary associations with business leadership is assumed to be economically efficient and more sensitive to client needs. Volunteering is approved, not because it is seen as an expression of religious virtue, but because it sustains an otherwise depleted social capital in civil society.

Volunteering stands in a relationship to wage labor that is necessary—just as atheism requires serious theism to have any vitality[40]—but the paradox of making the individual virtue of volunteering into a social institution contributes to its rationalization. In a modern society, volunteering is increasingly done by professional agencies, and in Britain a considerable component of their income is derived from the national lottery—an institution of which neither Baxter nor Wesley would have approved. Under such circumstances, it is difficult to argue that volunteering is a virtue.

Notes

1. Rotberg, 2001.
2. Nietzsche, 1973, p. 132.
3. Skocpol, 1999.
4. Veblen, 1994.
5. Veblen, 1994, p. 43.
6. Bourdieu, 1984.
7. Halfpenny, 2001.
8. Brown, Kenny, and Turner, 2000.
9. Wuthnow, 1996, p. 271.
10. Finch, 1989.
11. Weber, 1958, p. 206.
12. Turner, 1991, p. 89.
13. Kent, 2001, p. 212.
14. Scott and Stark, 1996.
15. Wetzel, 1992, p. 197.
16. Macedo, 1991, p. 274.
17. Tocqueville, 1968.
18. Crowley and Skocpol, 2000, p. 9.
19. Cohen and Rogers, 1995.
20. Bellah et al., 1985.
21. Wuthnow, 1991 and 1996.
22. Putnam, 1993 and 1995.
23. Halfpenny, 2001.
24. Abercrombie and Warde, 2000, p. 330.
25. Hirst, 1994.
26. Giner and Sarasa, 1996; Salamon and Anheier, 1999, p. 69.
27. Kendall and Knapp, 1996.
28. Galaskiewicz and Bielefeld, 1998, p. 35.
29. Stears, 1999.
30. Gold, 1971.
31. Turner, 2001.
32. Boli, 1991.
33. Lundström and Wijkström, 1998, pp. 46-51.
34. Brown, Kenny, and Turner, 2000.
35. Esping-Andersen, 1990.
36. Weber, 1978, pp. 579-589.
37. Weber, 1978, p. 580.
38. Weber, 1978, p. 585.
39. Weber, 1978, p. 589.
40. MacIntyre & Ricoeur, 1969.

9

The Relation between Independence and Trust

Emil Uddhammar

We are essentially social creatures, caught from the very beginning in a web of close relationships. At the same time we are individuals, struggling even as small children to express our individuality and to seek some autonomy. We cooperate every day with our families, at work, in the civic and religious associations of which we may be part, and also when we participate in economic exchange in various markets. At the end of the day we seek a refuge from all this—we try to get some private space, to "be ourselves" in our homes. Our individual lives could thus be described as two parallel rivers: one seeking cooperation and the other striving for independence.

In this chapter I shall discuss some basic conditions for cooperation and independence. I will argue that an assessment of the basic elements of social capital—networks, norms, and trust—is essential for understanding the preconditions of both cooperation and independence. Without networks, norms, and trust of a particular kind, independence or autonomy cannot be upheld, and certainly not cooperation. Networks and cooperation may be seen as aspects of the same idea. However, I will define people's networks as the actual realization of their cooperative endeavors.

I shall partly base my arguments on findings from an empirical research project I recently conducted, which involved open-ended interviews with 143 persons in four very different countries.[1] We asked these persons to describe their personal networks in their families, at work, in associations, and in politics. As such, networks can be of very different kinds. The characteristics of the actual networks we cooperate within should be able to say something about the preconditions for cooperation generally, for example in the economic and political arenas.

Our daily behavior is normally based upon the awareness of and respect for others. We try to give the person next to us on the commuter train some space to read his paper, and we do not throw offensive comments in the faces of our workmates. Such and similar rules constitute a minimum-level of value-premises of our ongoing cooperative activities. These value-premises are in part expectations from others—how we would like them to behave. But as our networks are interactive, they also reflect what others expect from us.

What kinds of networks do we cooperate within? What kinds of values and traits of character do we appreciate in our networks, what are the contents of the "minimum-level" of value premises of our daily social activities? To what extent could it be said that they are conducive to our capacity for independence?

A strong case has been made by authors such as Robert Putnam and Francis Fukuyama in support of the idea that formal membership in associations, and the "horizontal ties" that they are supposed to provide, are crucial for economic development and the functioning of democratic institutions. But I shall argue here that the very mechanisms that forge the link between formal membership in associations and economic and democratic performance have not been demonstrated convincingly. The theories on social capital often take the shape of a "black box"—not much is said on how associational membership results in a more efficient social exchange in other areas.

Eric Uslaner argues that there is no empirical evidence that organizational membership as such creates generalized trust, an important component of social capital.[2] Trust, he claims, is rather associated with an optimistic view of life. The "virtuous circles" that have been augmented in the recent debate do not create trust. More likely it is the "virtuous arrows" of good faith in others that add up to generalized trust, arrows that exist in persons in society, and that have been formed during childhood. Dietlind Stolle and Nancy Rosenblum have expressed a similar critique.[3]

Autonomy in Two Senses

The various forms of cooperation practiced throughout the history of mankind—and among our biological predecessors, the primates—have seldom been embedded in strong sentiments of respect for individual autonomy. Our social ties have often been caring and supportive, but almost always in a hierarchical setting. Our relational ties have, as a rule, not been based on the ethos of individual autonomy.

One might say that not even the most autocratic ruler is completely independent or autonomous in the long run. Dependencies are forged between the ruler and those subject to the rulings. Thus some relation, at least a mutual understanding, perhaps even mutual respect, may develop. In the relationship between lordship and bondage the seeds of self-consciousness were, according to Hegel, sown. In the confrontation between the slave and his master, the oppressed and the oppressor, ideas of individual autonomy and dreams of independence are born. Even hostages and captors develop social ties if time and circumstances allow it. Within terror groups it is therefore forbidden even to speak and have eye contact with hostages. With the tormented eye of the bondsman in sight, dangerous thoughts may start to grow.

Discussing autonomy, Joseph Raz has suggested that we should make a distinction between the *ideal of autonomy,* or autonomy in the primary sense, and our *real capacity for autonomy,* or autonomy in the secondary sense. Most of the time the ideal of autonomy may simply remain an ideal, since there are all sorts of physical, relational, and economic limitations to "perfect" autonomy.[4] Take, for example, the urge many teenagers have to become more independent from their parents. Even if a teenager would go to the extreme of running away from home, perhaps motivated by an urge to achieve the ideal of autonomy, it would most likely result only in a temporary state of independence. After a few days she would get hungry, and have to take a job or stay with some friend. She might feel independent if she took a job and earned her own money, but soon she would realize that *in reality* she would become dependent on her employer instead. If she sought further independence she could start her own business—but then she would become dependent on her customers. And so on. The perfect ideal of autonomy is thus incompatible with actual human relations in real life.

In most cases teenagers in opposition to their parents do not leave home. A normal individuation process takes place, which in turn prepares the adolescent for autonomy in the secondary sense. The teenager is allowed some leeway in clothing, political views, music style, etc., and through education she eventually becomes prepared for a more independent life, or autonomy in the second sense.

The Swedish sociologist Patrik Aspers (2000) has suggested that as we move between different arenas in our lives, this possibility of change also gives us a greater degree of independence or autonomy.

In his book *Rational Dependent Animals: Why Human Beings Need the Virtues* (1999), Alasdair MacIntyre has the same line of reasoning. As is evident in the title, Macintyre believes that we are "rational dependent animals." We are dependent as newborns, we are dependent when ill or handicapped, and we are dependent when old and feeble. MacIntyre wishes to abandon the focus on virtues of extraordinary performance and success, which he believes permeate our moral philosophical tradition.[5] In a good society, helpfulness, care, and mercy are qualities certainly as essential as enterprise, boldness, and courage. Each and every one of us may end up ill or handicapped, which is a strong argument for "the virtues of dependency." At the same time, MacIntyre emphasizes, our goal must be to develop an "independent practical reason."

In examining personal networks and the normative preconditions of the relationships within them, we would expect people who are active in modern economic regions and in the economically and politically most developed countries to show a greater appreciation of the virtues of independence and autonomy.

Networks and Norms

What is the relationship between virtues, social norms, and networks?

The Swedish ethicist Göran Möller defines virtues as *acquired character properties*. "We assimilate the virtues in a social context where several role models serve as examples worthy of imitation. We acquire our virtues from our surroundings, but little by little, as they have been internalized, they become part of our personality."[6] In acquiring a virtue, one's personality is formed by learning, socialization, "learning by doing," and some sort of disciplinary adaptation as described by Norbert Elias.

Social norms are defined by the late American sociologist James Coleman as follows: "A norm concerning a specific action exists when the socially defined right to control the action is held not by the actor but by others." The amount of authority needed in order for a group of people to enforce such a norm "is created by the social consensus that placed the right in their hands." [7] Norms are social constructs and can be upheld only by sanctions, i.e. praise (benefits) or blame (costs) in an ongoing social exchange. Traffic regulations are typical examples. You follow them strictly as long as there is an obvious risk of getting caught, but get very liberal when you realize that the risk of sanctions is low. Queuing is another. It is socially unthinkable to jump a queue in a bank in any country or in a Swedish liquor store. If you do, you will immediately be exposed to various unpleasant and rather harsh social sanctions.

Coleman makes another important observation:

> [The presence of norms] results in higher levels of satisfaction—though perhaps at the cost of reducing the satisfaction of some members whose actions are most constrained by the norms. Their absence allows individuals to realize greater satisfaction from their own actions, but leaves them with less satisfaction over all, as they suffer from the unconstrained actions of others. [8]

The argument has wide implications. Basically, it says that the degree to which a social norm infringes upon your freedom of movement—your independence—is proportional to the satisfaction you will get from the overall social predictability that the prevalence of that norm will give in society. An example: Granted that a sufficient proportion of the grown-up population in your town has properly queued in line at the bank a sufficient number of times, you can rest quite assured that when you pay a visit there next time there will not be a fight or a bidding deciding who will be first to the cashier.

In the field of network analysis, Clyde J. Mitchell suggests that we separate the communicative content in the links in a particular network from the ongoing exchange as such, which in turn should be separated from the normative content of the links. A methodological guide to network analysis says: "Social network analysis is based upon an assumption of the importance of relationships among interacting units."[9] The focus is on relational concepts and processes and the analysis unit is, according to Wasserman and Faust, "not the individual but an entity consisting of a collection of individuals and the linkages among them."

In our interviews, we chose to ask people about the importance and significance of their own informal network relations. Our analytical unit was the individual, but in a secondary sense also the links between the individuals and the normative content of these links.

In his definition of social capital, James Coleman discusses networks of relationships between two or more individuals. "Social capital...is created when relations between individuals are changed in a direction that facilitates action,"[10] and further on: "The function identified through the concept of social capital is the resource that a social structure constitutes for the actors involved, in that it can be used to realize their interests."[11]

A friendly exchange may, according to a famous classification by Aristotle, firstly be of a utilitarian nature, as in business transactions. It may secondly be a pleasurable exchange of feelings—as between a couple in love, or between a mother and her child. It may finally also be a deeper relationship between adult equals aimed at lasting friendship and joint community in the good life.

Take the following scenario as an example of how informal network relationships may evolve: Four parents, who have never met before, find themselves talking to each other outside the home of their shared daycare provider on the their children's first day there. The conversation begins pleasantly, perhaps with neutral small talk about the weather, or about how well their children seem to be doing. Questions are soon bandied about the group. The questions are answered and counter-questions placed. After the meeting, the parents know something of each other, and something of the children. The meeting and the conversation still have the nature of a formal network, characterized by the institutional contact with the caregiver, who fills a utilitarian function for each family individually, but also a common utilitarian function, since the children have fun together and everyone can identify this.

After a few weeks, we assume that the four parents have exchanged further information—they learn more and more about each other. They may begin to help each other out by performing small favors. One of them takes the other's child to or from the caregiver's home on certain days, another on other days. At this stage, it soon becomes apparent whether the mechanism of reciprocal altruism—the implicit agreement that if you will help me, I will help you another time—is developing or not. Will the formal relationship become a mutually fruitful network?

Assume that one parent never returns favors, but at first is happy to accept the help of the others without further explanation. Eventually, an imbalance arises that will feel troublesome to all four. It is highly likely that the three parents who return favors regularly will begin to talk about how the fourth parent does not.

The dynamics of the described network is illustrated graphically in Figure 1 (below). The strength of the network is proportional to the thickness of the lines connecting the individuals. At the point in

Figure 1

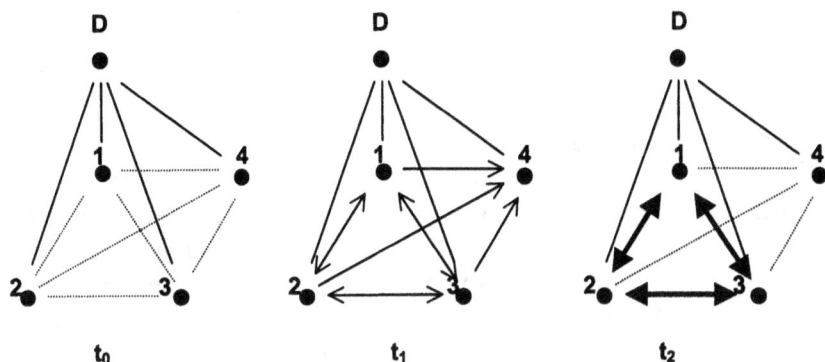

t_0 t_1 t_2

time t_0, only formal relations exist between parents 1–4 and caregiver D, and relations among the parents are practically undeveloped. In phase t_1, mutuality among the parents is examined. The asymmetry of the exchange between on the one hand individuals 1–3 and on the other individual 4 leads to the progressive weakening of relations with individual 4. At t_2, a pattern has crystallized: parents 1–3 have reinforced their reciprocal exchange, while parent 4 is no longer included in the network. The formal tie to the caregiver remains unchanged. Eventually, "relations between individuals are changed in a direction that facilitates action," and social capital in the Coleman sense has arisen among parents 1–3. The reason is, that they, *by practical action*, have demonstrated helpfulness and reliability.

Parents 1–3 have created a firm foundation for trust that is valuable to all three in many ways. They can count on further help and support in future. They may think about how, when the children start school, there will be the advantage of each child already having a good relationship with the other children in the group and to the parents, and so on. Note that the advantage that each of parents 1–3 gains from the reinforced network is at once individual—each gains greater self-confidence, taking note that s/he can create trusting relationships—and social—each notices that s/he can both get *and* give help.

But what can we say about parent 4? We can think of various scenarios, perhaps that she had a network of her own, or a grandparent that could help her out. Irrespective of this, the important fact in this example is the asymmetry created. From a normative and reciprocal-altruistic standpoint, the fourth person "excommunicates" herself from the reciprocal-altruistic community of the three others—through her independence. We may say that independence has its price.

In this example, we have assumed that not independence, but other virtues, such as helpfulness, reliability, and loyalty, contributed to a joint facilitation of future structured action. The exchange of information was another important factor. Such an exchange—like the constant small talk and sharing of gossip about what is happening in the group of children and among the parents from our example—seems to have an important catalytic function among higher primates. According to Dunbar (1998), this need for information arose from the need to create small alliances within larger groups, in order to maintain balance in the larger group. According to this theory, primates were developing small islands of social capital even before the evolution of language, and the need for more information about the others in the group may have been a driving force behind that development.[12]

All human interaction begins from a position of uncertainty and lack of information about what kind of people the others are and what they are planning to do. In the example with the parents, they know that the others have children placed under the supervision of the same caregiver, but not much more. The rational reaction upon such an occasion is to seek information about the others, which is most easily accomplished by starting up a conversation. William Galston identifies this particular ability—to seek information, to keep oneself up to date—as an important quality—a modern virtue. This is of course not only for reasons that have to do with one's own interests, but also because many of the qualities we value in people are predicated upon empathy and genuine interest in other people.

We have thus seen that several factors converge in facilitating structures of future cooperation—information exchange, behavior according to reciprocal expectations, and future expectations of similar behavior: trust.

We can also say that our capacity for autonomy is dependent upon a structure of expectations for others—that they will behave according to certain norms. If I cannot expect that people will behave in a reasonably orderly fashion with regard to any particular activity—e.g., if there is a plausible risk that I will have to get involved in a fight in order to be able to withdraw my money every time I visit the bank—I would have to depend on a number of other people to protect me, and thus dramatically increase my time costs as well as real costs of that activity.

The Structure of Our Networks

Most of us are indeed engaged in relational undertakings daily. In our sample in all four countries—Sweden, New Zealand, Thailand, and Kenya—everyone had some family connections, and only 4 percent didn't have a work network. With 70 percent having contacts within some voluntary organization, this also looks like a rather healthy sector.

When we compared the countries, we found that the respondents in Sweden, with the highest GNP per capita, also have the largest share of partakers in the voluntary sector—89 percent. However, in Thailand, more than 50 percent of our sample had no connections within the sector. Kenya, by far the poorest country in the sample, had the next highest voluntary sector participation rate.

When we compared the structure of the family and work networks of our informants, the most significant relation was found between the size and average closeness of work network contacts and economic region. People in high-tech areas have significantly more persons in their work network than those in other regions. Contacts are also significantly less close and more indirect (phone or mail) in the high-tech regions, whereas contacts at work are significantly more in-person in the least developed regions.[13] The same pattern goes for education: people with a university education have more people in their networks, and communicate less frequently and in a more indirect way with them.

Regarding family networks, size differences between economic regions are not significant. The most extensive family networks were recorded in Sweden and New Zealand. The frequencies of contacts were higher in Thailand, and the number of indirect vs. direct contacts within family networks was much higher in high-tech regions than in regions with traditional industries.

If we put these pieces together, we find that economic development seems to go hand in hand with a large number of persons in the work network, with whom one often has indirect contact, and not necessarily on a daily basis.

Conditions for Trust

Interpersonal and generalized trust has been described in the recent debate as one of the most important factors that facilitate social and economic cooperation. Trust may thus be directed to a group or a number of known individuals, or to anyone, known or unknown, in a particular society.[14] According to the economists Ronald Coase and Douglass C. North, a high level of generalized trust helps to bring down the "transaction costs" in the economy. If we are confident that the plumber whom we have hired is honest and competent, we may leave a hidden key to him so that we can go to work as usual when he does his installation. We may recollect the example of the four parents, and say that their interpersonal social action in general was facilitated by the trust they gradually developed. In the latter example there was definitely less trust in the beginning than at the end—and at that point also some mistrust.

As an employee, consumer, or business owner, a person attaches a certain confidence to particular determined currencies, a lender, or a borrower. Well-known credit cards, that have been certified as reliable and which have empirically worked well, may be used as a currency in the most varied of environments. They communicate confidence and information about creditworthiness reminiscent of that which one can gather in the local society's network, but function more discreetly and anonymously.[15] Famous brands also instill confidence in the consumer to a varying degree. SAS and Lufthansa generally have a better reputation than Aeroflot. Mercedes and Volvo generally have a better reputation than Lada. Subjective judgments certainly prevail in the market, but some brands and credit functions generally have a higher trust capital than others.

According to the *World Value Survey*,[16] which is based on national surveys in forty-three countries, 65 percent of the Swedes surveyed said that "you can trust most people." Kenya is not part of the study, but the corresponding figure for Nigeria is 23 percent and for South Africa 27 percent. Thailand was not part of that study either, but in China 50 percent answered in the affirmative, and in India and South Korea 42 percent said that they trust most people. Inglehart has shown that there is a correlation between generalized trust and a stable democracy.[17]

In her classic study, *Governing the Commons* (1990), Ostrom underlines the importance of norms in creating trust and cooperation. People who live close to a commons used by all tend to develop strong shared norms in the mutual social exchanges in which they partake. One of her examples is how a local fishing area, close to the shore in Sri Lanka, can be used. People who live there have developed mutual respect, but this does not include the big trawlers that occasionally come by and troll the fishing area. The reason is not only the size of the trawlers and their much larger capacity:

> Often the operators of trawlers live elsewhere, belong to different ethnic or racial groups, and share few of the local norms of behavior. They do not drink in the same bars, their families do not live in the nearby fishing villages, and they are not involved in the same network of relationships that depend on the establishment of a reputation for keeping promises and accepting the norms of the local community regarding behavior.[18]

According to Ostrom, it is crucial for one's reputation and trustworthiness to belong to a "network of relationships." But this raises another important question: How can links of trust be forged between different local area networks, where trusting relationships already exist? How can we include "the others" in the web of trust? How can we move from local trust to general trust, and what is the general relation between the two kinds of trust?

In our study, one of the first questions in our guide was similar: "Generally, do you trust other people?" In fact, we got very high percentages of "yes" in Sweden and Thailand: 96 and 90 percent. There is a gap to New Zealand's 67 percent and Kenya's 60 percent.

Women were less inclined to accept generalized trust: 66 percent answered in the affirmative compared to 83 percent of the men. We found no significant differences on trust when we grouped the sample according to occupational level, marital status, religious activity, or educational level.

Then we asked, "When you think about persons you can trust, can you describe what it is that makes you trust him or her?" One typical answer came from a middle-aged woman in New Zealand: "Well I trust my mother. I suppose she's been there for me since my birth, you know, no matter what I've done she's always stood by me."[19] Or a young woman in Thailand: "Like the people in my family, I am able to trust them because we have grown up together and know each other."[20]

Many answers were about a person's ability to keep information— to be able to entrust. "A trustful person should keep a secret. I realize who can be trusted from what I have learnt from them in the past. They have never disappointed me or let me down before," said a young woman in Bangkok. "Because they are honest, they keep their words" (young woman in Nairobi). "My permanent customer— I trust him because he comes, gives me an order, and leaves money behind as payment for the order" (another young woman in Nairobi).

"Well, take my friend Solveig that I trust, we have known each other very long." [Why do you trust her?] "Well, because she is a very honest person and because she always stood by me if I needed help, she never let me down," said a woman in Bracke, Sweden. A middle-aged man in Invercargill, New Zealand said: "Sincerity. I think if they seem genuinely sincere in what they are doing and that they want me to trust them. Also their performance, if they, if I see that they have actually achieved what they've said they are going to do, set out to do, then I believe that they'll continue to do that and gain my trust."

Some answers stressed that if there was a strong friendship since the school years, for example, you may not need to meet very often; you know that you will get help if need be. One woman in New Zealand, who is an active Christian, said that she preferred to trust people in different ways. She did not at all trust some of her family members with material goods, simply because they would not return them or would break them, but she trusted them all and completely in matters of family loyalty, caring, and love. Others stressed body language: "Time will have to show, but you can also feel it, I think. You can feel it pretty well. If you can look them in the eye and get a solid handshake, then you can trust them" (Middle-aged man, Sweden). "Well I just think that they look at you, they can look you in the eye, I think is 90 percent of it, you know...I just look at a person" (older man, Invercargill, New Zealand).

The answers show a pattern of four main factors that tend to inspire confidence and trust:

- the time you have known a person;
- relational ties: siblings, parents;
- if a person can stand a "test" that you arrange, for example:

  —the ability to keep information—not passing it on;

  —if a person carries out what you both had agreed upon;
- if a person is helpful and friendly.

Generalized trust has the advantage of facilitating cooperation. But as a feature of a given society, trust is not a static commodity.

The changes in the world economy after September 11, 2001 is a dramatic example of how the general level of trust affects us all, but also how it can be changed almost overnight. The terror acts have had widespread and dramatic effects on our behavior in travel and consumption patterns. They have also resulted in a vast number of layoffs at airports, airlines, and other businesses connected with travel and tourism.

Another example of how our level of general trust could be dramatically altered is when I passed a fairly small street in our quiet neighborhood in Uppsala one evening. I noticed a car passing at a very high speed, probably more than 80 mph. The car crossed a bigger road close by—against red light and amid crossing traffic—without slowing down the slightest bit. At that point I got really chilled, and felt the adrenaline flowing into my veins. This is mad behavior, I thought, the driver is not even concerned for his own life! The driver not only broke the law in a flagrant way, he also seemed utterly irrational.

The next day I read in the local paper that a drug-addicted driver had been caught nearby, and arrested. As I thought that this must have been the driver I saw last night, I was calmed. If this *were* the only "mad driver," my basic expectations about the future would not have to be changed. Had I noted more drivers behaving in the same unexpected way, my distrustfulness would have increased. Had more and more "mad drivers" cropped up, that would most certainly have affected my own and other people's behavior very decisively. I would have warned family and friends, and our general confidence or trust would have been dramatically lowered.

A given society's level of "generalized trust" can thus easily be changed. In fact, it is constantly dependent on all the small signs and behaviors of others that we observe and register every day, even every minute. We "translate" these observations—almost without thinking about it—to either an approval, or an alarm signal. If we do not observe these common regularities in the behavior of others, if some grave disturbance or irregularity occurs—fighting in the bank queue, airplanes hitting skyscrapers, cars driven at very high speed with no consideration for the driver's own or other people's safety—we react very firmly by radically lowering, or even completely withdrawing, our general trust.

If our society were to reach such a state, we would become much more dependent upon the particular trust we have in the particular persons we have particular knowledge about. Thus we can see that generalized trust among a given society's members is positively related to their real capacity for independence.

What We Like in Others

But what character traits do we appreciate in the people with whom we cooperate? The answer to that question is of course very individual, and when I relate the answers of the persons we have interviewed it should be remembered that the sample is small and does not permit generalizations at large. However, a strategic sample can give us hints that we can use in generating hypotheses that could be tested in other studies.

Early in the interview, before any specific values or virtues had been named, we asked for "three character qualities that you value in people you deal with." In the table below, all three have been included, though some did not mention more than two, or even one.

It is possible to separate a few different types of character traits among the answers given. First, we have the "hard reciprocal core" virtues: honesty and reliability. They are obviously the most popular, and ranked the highest or very high in most countries. Interestingly enough this is not the case in Thailand, where "friendly" is the most popular. However, at second place also in Thailand is reliability. We may thus conjecture that the reciprocal virtues of honesty and reliability are universally strongly demanded character qualities that we want to see in people with whom we deal.

Table 1
"Name three character traits that you particularly appreciate in people you are dealing with." First six mentioned in rank order. Maximum value 100%; all three traits mentioned included.

New Zealand	Thailand	Kenya	Sweden	All
Honest	Friendly	Honest	Reliable	Honest
84%	24%	59%	35%	53%
Integrity	Reliable	Friendly	Honest	Reliable
22%	24%	26%	30%	23%
Reliable	Direct	Hard working	Self- confident	Direct
20%	21%	23%	30%	15%
Direct	Helpful	Trustworthy	Trustworthy	Trustworthy
18%	17%	23%	20%	14%
Friendly	Honest	Dedicated	Honest	Friendly
18%	17%	21%	15%	12%
Humor	Cheerful	Reliable	Hard- working	Dedicated
13%	14%	21%	15%	11%
(45)	(30)	(40)	(28)	(143=n)

Secondly, we have the "helpful" virtues: friendliness, being help-ful, and kindness. These are particularly valued among the Thai, but also among the Kenyans.

We also find some distinct "virtues of independence" highly ranked, among them integrity, directness, and self-confidence. To be self-confident and to have integrity are highly regarded virtues in New Zealand and Sweden. "Directness" ranked third in the whole sample.

In the fourth category we find the "industrious" virtues, particu-larly valued in Kenya, with "hard-working" ranked third. This is ranked sixth in Sweden.

Last but not least we should mention the more joyful virtues of humor and cheerfulness, most popular in New Zealand and Thai-land. Perhaps I should add that they are also mentioned by the Swedes, but lower down in the list...

But if we look at the first character qualities mentioned in the participants' answers (i.e. they did not include all three we asked for), we get a slightly different picture. The idea of such an analysis is that the one that first comes to a person's mind is also the single most important one. In this analysis, their positions were more promi-nent in the "hard reciprocal core" of character traits. In Thailand honesty climbed to third rank, and in the whole sample honesty is even more conspicuously singled out as leader of the "most wanted" list.

Conclusion

What we have seen here is that our empirical study confirms Coleman's thesis that shared norms of reciprocity increases the overall predictability of a given social environment. This predictability can-not of course be taken too far—that would take us to a Spartan soci-ety or worse. But what kinds of norms, then, are conducive to a reasonable type of predictability, which increases our real capacity for autonomy?

Our empirical study gives clear indications that these norms are of three kinds: the "hard reciprocal core" character traits of honesty and reliability, the "helpful" norms of friendliness, being helpful, and being kind, and the "industrious" ethics of hard work and dedi-cation. These are the norms that the persons in our networks them-selves mentioned as the most important in the people they deal with in their daily networks. It should be safe to assume that our informants would not focus on character traits in others that infringe upon their own real capacity for autonomy.

We have found that our capacity for generalized trust is linked to similar norms, particularly to the "hard reciprocal core" and the "helpful." We have also seen that generalized trust is not a fixed commodity in society. It is safe to assume that in an environment that is dominated by the norms mentioned, the "arrows of trust" (Uslaner) that we normally get during childhood will fly on through our lives. But these norms can become inert with short notice. We daily "read" a multitude of small signs that people whom we meet in our homes, on the street, at work, etc. send out. We check to see whether or not they correspond with the basic norms of reciprocity and helpfulness that form the very core of our trustful relationships. If they don't, we are quick to switch from a high level of generalized trust to a very limited one. In a state of increasing violence, for example, we would retreat to the persons we have the longest historical knowledge of, and whom we "know" we may trust. In such a state, our real capacity for autonomy would be dramatically decreased.

Appendix

Our case involves an international comparison, where we enter differences in culture, religion, economic performance, and politics. However, the study also includes a comparison between three regional types, characterized respectively by (a) a thriving traditional manufacturing industry with low unemployment, (b) a booming information technology industry, and (c) an area dominated by a traditional manufacturing industry but suffering from a long recession and high unemployment.

The design and method chosen did not allow a randomly selected and representative population. The sub-groups of informants were therefore selected strategically to get maximum variation according to age, position in the hierarchy, and sex.

As the number of informants in each region was limited due to time and cost constraints, we could not hope to reach any final causal conclusions. We can, however, say something on how networks function at the micro level, and will be able to investigate how the function of networks corresponds to democratic and economic performance.

Apart from Sweden, which was selected on the merit of being the home base of the research program itself, and often conceived to be one of the most modern and socially-advanced countries, we sought to select other countries that differed significantly according to certain cultural, social, and political indicators. A detailed table specifying the indicators is found in Uddhammar and Erixon, 2002, page 69.

The regions selected in southern Sweden were Gnosjö-Anderstorp-Värnamo—a booming area with small, traditional manufacturing. As approximately corresponding regions we selected Christchurch in New Zealand, Thika Town in Kenya, and Chiang Mai in Thailand. As a region with high unemployment and long-time recession we chose Bräcke in northern Sweden, and to correspond with it Ayuttaya in Thailand, two suburbs of Nairobi—Buru-Buru Rabai Road and Muthurwa-Kamakunji—and Invercargill on the south island of New Zealand. As booming areas with a major presence of high-tech industries we selected Kista, north of Stockholm, Bangkok in Thailand, Nairobi in Kenya, and Auckland in New Zealand.

Notes

1.   I will use data that we have collected through network mapping and structured but open-ended interviews with 143 strategically selected individuals in three different economic regions in four very different countries. The comparative method we used aimed at finding as different countries as possible, but also at trying to find rather similarly structured regions within each country.
2.   Uslaner, 2000–01, pp. 569–90.
3.   Stolle, 1998, p. 500; Rosenblum, 1998.
4.   Raz, 1986, pp. 369–78.
5.   The Norwegian theologian Ivar Asheim has argued that the virtue ethics of antiquity was far too rational and individual. In his opinion, it is only when the individual and social aspects confirm one another that virtue ethics achieve a sound foundation.
6.   Möller, 1998, p. 27.
7.   Coleman, 1990, pp. 242–43.
8.   Coleman, 1987, pp. 133–55. This quote: p. 153.
9.   Wasserman and Faust, 1994, p. 4.
10.   Coleman, 1990, p. 304.
11.   Coleman, 1990, p. 305.
12.   Dunbar, 1998.
13.   The directional measure Lambda for "work network closeness grouped" by "region" (dependent variable) is 0.193, significant at the 0.0001 level.
14.   See Yamagishi and Yamagishi, 1994, pp. 129–66.
15.   See Klein, 1997, p. 285: "In a [vast society like the United States] the credit bureau plays a role that gossip plays in a small community, although in a much more discreet fashion."
16.   Inglehart, 1997, p. 399
17.   Inglehart, 1997, p. 227.
18.   Ostrom, 1990, p. 206.
19.   Interview no. 26.
20.   Interview no. 53. The following quotes derive from interviews no. 53, 103, 114, 129, 40, 139, and 39.

References

Abercrombie, Nicholas and Alan Warde (eds.), 2000, *Contemporary British Society*. Cambridge: Polity Press.

Annas, Julia, 1993, *The Morality of Happiness*. Oxford: Oxford University Press.

Aristotle, 1984, *Rhetoric*, in *The Complete Works of Aristotle*, Jonathan Barnes (ed.). Princeton, NJ: Princeton University Press.

Baker, K. M., 1975, *Condorcet: From Natural Philosophy to Social Mathematics*. Chicago: University of Chicago Press.

Barry, Brian, 1995, *Justice as Impartiality*. Oxford: Clarendon Press.

Beauchamp, Tom, 1991, "Competence," in *Competency: A Study of Informal Competency Determinations in Primary Care*, Mary Ann Gardell Cutter et al. (eds.). Dordrecht: Kluwer.

Beckman, Ludvig, 2001, *The Liberal State and the Politics of Virtue*. New Brunswick, NJ: Transaction Publishers.

Bellah, Robert, et al., 1985, *Habits of the Heart: Individualism and Commitment in Public Life*. Berkeley, CA: University of California Press.

Beretta. Ilva, 1993, *The World is a Garden: Garden Poetry of the English Renaissance*. Uppsala: Almqvist & Wiksell International (Studia Anglistica Upsaliensia 84).

Berkowitz, Peter, 1999, *Virtue and the Making of Modern Liberalism*. Princeton, NJ: Princeton University Press.

Berlin, Isaiah, 1969, *Four Essays on Liberty*. Oxford: Oxford University Press.

Berofsky, Bernard, 1995, *Liberation From Self: A Theory of Personal Autonomy*. Cambridge: Cambridge University Press.

Boli, John, 1991, "Sweden: is there a viable third sector?" in *Between States and Markets*, Robert Wuthnow (ed.), Princeton, NJ: Princeton University Press.

Bostock, David, 2001, *Aristotle's Ethics*. Oxford: Oxford University Press.

Bourdieu, Pierre, 1984, *Distinction: A Social Critique of the Judgement of Taste*. London: Routledge and Kegan Paul.

Braybrooke, David, 1998, *Moral Objectives, Rules, and the Forms of Social Change*. Toronto: University of Toronto Press.

Brissot, J-P., 1911, *Correspondance et papiers*. Ed. C. Perround. Paris: Picard et fils.

Brown, Kevin, Susan Kenny, and Bryan S. Turner, 2000, *Rhetorics of Welfare: Uncertainty, Choice and Voluntary Associations*. Basingstoke: Macmillan.

Carlson, P., 1998, "Self-Perceived Health in East and West Europe: Another European Health Divide," in *Social Science & Medicine*, 46:1355-66.

Carruthers, Peter and Peter K. Smith (eds.), 1996, *Theories of Theories of Mind*, Cambridge: Cambridge University Press.

Clor, Harry, 1985, "Mill and Millians on Liberty and Moral Character," in *The Review of Politics*, vol. 47.

Cobban, A., 1971, *Aspects of the French Revolution*. London: Paladin.

Cohen, G. A., 1997, "Where the action is: On the site of distributive justice," in *Philosophy and Public Affairs*, vol. 26.

—, 2000, *If You're an Egalitarian, How Come You're so Rich?* Cambridge, MA: Harvard University Press.

Cohen, Joshua and Joel Rogers (eds.), 1995, *Associations and Democracy*. London: Verso.

Coleman, James S., 1987, "Norms as Social Capital," in *Economic Imperialism: The Economic Approach Applied Outside the Field of Economics*, G. Radnitzky and P. Bernholz (eds.). New York: Paragon House.

—, 1990, *Foundations of Social Theory*. Cambridge, MA: Harvard University Press.

Condorcet, Marie Jean Antoine Nicolas Caritat, marquis de, 1786, *Vie de Turgot*, vol. 5 of Condorcet O'Connor, A. and M.F. Arago (eds.), 1847-49.

Condorcet O'Connor, A. and M-F Arago (eds.), 1847-49, *Oeuvres*. 12 vols. Paris.

Cook, Maeve, 1997, "Authenticity and Autonomy: Taylor, Habermas and the Politics of Recognition," in *Political Theory*, vol. 25.

Crisp, Roger and Michael Slote (eds.), 1997, *Virtue Ethics*. Oxford: Oxford University Press.

Crowley, J. E. and Theda Skocpol, 2000, "The Rush to Organize: Explaining Associational Formation in the United States, 1860s–1920s." Unpublished conference paper. Washington, DC: American Political Science Association.

Currie, Gregory, 1997, "The Paradox of Caring: Fiction and the Philosophy of Mind," in *Emotion and the Arts*, Mette Hjort and Sue Laver (eds.). New York: Oxford University Press.

—, 1995a, "Imagination and Simulation: Aesthetics Meets Cognitive Science," in Davies & Stone (eds.), 1995b.

—, 1995b, "The Moral Psychology of Fiction," in *Australasian Journal of Philosophy*, vol. 73.

—, 1996, "Simulation-Theory, Theory-Theory and the Evidence from Autism," in Carruthers & Smith (eds.), 1996.

—, 1998. "Realism of Character and the Value of Fiction," in *Aesthetics and Ethics: Essays at the Intersection*, Jerrold Levinson (ed.). Cambridge: Cambridge University Press.

Dan-Cohen, Meir, 1992, "Conceptions of Choice and Conceptions of Autonomy," in *Ethics*, vol. 102.

Darwall, Stephen, 1999, "Sympathetic liberalism: Recent work on Adam Smith," in *Philosophy and Public Affairs*, vol. 28.

Davies, Martin and Tony Stone (eds.), 1995a, *Folk Psychology: The Theory of Mind Debate*. Oxford: Blackwell.

— and Tony Stone (eds.), 1995b, *Mental Simulation: Evaluations and Applications*. Oxford: Blackwell.

Depré, Carole, 1991, "The Meaning of Home: Literature Review and Directions for Future Research and Theoretical Development," in *Journal of Architecture and Planning Research*, no. 2.

Dunbar, Robin, 1998, *Grooming, Gossip, and the Evolution of Language*. Cambridge, MA: Harvard University Press.

Dunn, John (ed.), 1992, *Democracy: The Unfinished Journey*. Oxford: Oxford University Press.

— (ed.), 1990, *The Economic Limits to Modern Politics*. Cambridge: Cambridge University Press.

—, 1980, *Political Obligation in its Historical Context*. Cambridge: Cambridge University Press.

—, 1985, *Rethinking Modern Political Theory*. Cambridge: Cambridge University Press.

—, 1990, *Interpreting Political Responsibility*. Cambridge: Polity Press.

—, 1996, *The History of Political Theory*. Cambridge: Cambridge University Press.

—, 2000, *The Cunning of Unreason*. London: HarperCollins.

Dworkin, Gerald, 1988, *The Theory and Practice of Autonomy*. Cambridge: Cambridge University Press.

Dworkin, Ronald, 1977, *Taking Rights Seriously.* London: Duckworth.

—, 1990, "Foundations of Liberal Equality," in *The Tanner Lectures on Human Values*, Grethe B. Peterson (ed.). Logan, UT: Utah State University Press.

—, 2000, *Sovereign Virtue.* Cambridge, MA: Harvard University Press.

Elam, Katarina, 2001, *Emotions as a Mode of Understanding: An Essay in Philosophical Aesthetics.* Diss., Uppsala: Department of ALM, Aesthetics and Cultural Studies.

Ellis, H.E., 1989, "Montesquieu's Modern Politics: The Spirit of the Laws and the Problem of Modern Monarchy in Old Regime France," in *History of Political Thought*, vol. 10.

Esping-Andersen, Gösta, 1990, *The Three Worlds of Welfare Capitalism.* Cambridge: Polity Press.

Estlund, David, 1998, "Liberalism, Equality and Fraternity in Cohen's Critique of Rawls," in *Journal of Political Philosophy*, vol. 6.

Faber, Marvin, 1947-48, "Modes of Reflection," in *Philosophy and Phenomenological-Research*, vol. 8.

Finch, Janet, 1989, *Family Obligations and Social Change.* Cambridge: Polity Press.

Flanagan, Owen, 1990, "Identity and Strong Evaluation," in *Identity, Character and Morality: Essays in Moral Psychology*, Owen Flanagan and Amélie Oksenberg Rorty (eds.). Cambridge, MA: The MIT Press.

Fontana, Biancamaria (ed.), 1994, *The Invention of the Modern Republic.* Cambridge: Cambridge University Press.

Forsyth, M., 1989, *Pierre-Louis Roederer: The Spirit of the Revolution of 1789 and Other Writings of the Revolutionary Epoch.* Aldershot: Scolar Press.

Foucault, Michel, 1975, *Surveiller et punir.* Paris: Gallimard.

—, 1981–90, *The History of Sexuality.* Vols. 1-3. Harmondsworth: Penguin.

—, 2001, *Power.* Ed. J. de Faubion. Harmondsworth: Penguin.

Frankfurt, Harry, 1971, "Freedom of the Will and the Concept of a Person," in *Journal of Philosophy*, vol. 67.

—, 1999. "Equality and Respect," in *Necessity, Volition, and Love.* Cambridge: Cambridge University Press.

Freeman, Michael, 1993, *Rewriting the Self: History, Memory, Narrative.* London: Routledge.

Fukuyama, Francis, 1992, *The End of History and the Last Man.* London: Hamish Hamilton.

Galaskiewicz, Joseph and Wolfgang Bielefeld, 1998, *Nonprofit Organizations in an Age of Uncertainty: A Study of Organizational Change.* New York: Aldine de Gruyter.

Galston, William, 1988, "Liberal virtues," in *American Political Science Review*, vol. 82.

Geuss, Raymond, 1980, *The Idea of a Critical Theory.* Cambridge: Cambridge University Press.

—, 2000, "Virtue and the Good Life," in *Arion*, vol. 4.

—, 2001, *History and Illusion in Politics.* Cambridge: Cambridge University Press.

Gilbert, Ryle, 1952, *The Concept of Mind.* London: Hutchinson.

Giner, Salvador and S. Sarasa, 1996. "Civic Altruism and Social Policy," in *International Sociology*, vol. 11.

Gold, D. B., 1971, "Women and Volunteerism," in *Woman in Sexist Society*, Vivian Gornick and Barbara K. Moran (eds.). New York: Basic Books.

Goodenough, Ursula and Paul Woodruff, 2001, "Mindful Virtue, Mindful Reverence," in *Zygon* (forthcoming).

Grotius, Hugo, 1925, *De jure belli ac pacis libritres.* Oxford: Clarendon Press.

Gueniffey, P., 1994, "Cordeliers and Girondins: the Prehistory of the Republic," in B. Fontana (ed.).

Gustafsson, Gerhard, 1991, *Landscape, the Individual and Society: Change, Meanings, and Goals.* Karlstad: University of Karlstad (Research report 91:14.).

Gwartney, James D. et al., 2000, *Economic Freedom of the World: 2000 Annual Report.* Vancouver, BC: The Fraser Institute.

Halfpenny, Peter, 2001, "Philanthropy: A Sociological Analysis." Paper presented to the *British Sociological Association, Jubilee Conference.* Manchester: University of Manchester.

Halliwell, Stephen, 1986, *Aristotle's Poetics.* London: Duckworth.

Hampson, N., 1988, "La Patrie," in Lucas, (ed.) 1988.

—, 1991, *Saint-Just.* Oxford: Blackwell.

Harman, Gilbert, 2000, *Explaining Value and Other Essays in Moral Philosophy.* Oxford: Oxford University Press.

Haydon, C. and W. Doyle, (eds.), 1999, *Robespierre.* Cambridge, Cambridge University Press.

Held, David et al., 1999, *Global Transformations: Politics, Economics and Culture.* Cambridge: Polity.

Higgonet, Patrice, 1998, *Goodness beyond Virtue: Jacobins during the French Revolution.* Cambridge, MA: Harvard University Press.

Hill, Thomas E., 1991, *Autonomy and Self-Respect.* Cambridge: Cambridge University Press.

Hirst, Paul Q., 1994, *Associative Democracy.* Cambridge: Polity Press.

Hont, I. and M. Ignatieff (eds.), 1983, *Wealth and Virtue.* Cambridge: Cambridge University Press.

Hütter, Reinhard, 1998, "The Twofold Center of Lutheran Ethics; Christian Freedom and God's Commandments," in *The Promise of Lutheran Ethics*, Karen L. Bloomquist and John R. Summe (eds.). Minneapolis, MN: Fortress Press.

Inglehart, Ronald, 1997, *Modernization and Postmodernization: Cultural, Economic, and Political Change in 43 Societies.* Princeton, NJ: Princeton University Press.

Ivanhoe, Philip J., 1990, *Ethics in the Confucian Tradition: The Thought of Mencius and Wang Yang-Ming.* Atlanta: Scholars Press.

—, 2000, *Confucian Moral Self-Cultivation.* 2nd ed. Indianapolis, IN: Hackett Publishing Co.

Jaume, L., 1989, *Le discours Jacobin et la démocratie.* Paris: Fayard.

Jaurès, J., 1968, *Histoire socialiste de la Révolution française.* Paris: Éditions Sociales.

Johnson, Mark, 1993, *Moral Imagination: Implications of Cognitive Science for Ethics.* Chicago: The University of Chicago Press.

Jones, Peter, 1994, *Rights.* London: Macmillan.

Kane, Robert, 1996, *Through the Moral Maze.* Armonk, NY: New Castle Books.

Kates, G., 1985, *The Cercle Social, The Girondins, and the French Revolution.* Princeton, NJ: Princeton University Press.

Kendall, Jeremy and Martin Knapp, 1996, *The Voluntary Sector in the United Kingdom.* Manchester: Manchester University Press.

Kent, Bonnie, 2001, "Augustine's Ethic," in *The Cambridge Companion to Augustine.* Cambridge: Cambridge University Press.

Keohane, N.O., 1980, *Philosophy and the State in France: The Renaissance to the Enlightenment.* Princeton, NJ: Princeton University Press.

Kerby, Anthony Paul, 1986, "The Language of the Self," in *Philosophy Today*, vol. 30.

—, 1991, *Narrative and the Self.* Indianapolis, IN: Indiana University Press.

Kertzer, David I., 1988, *Ritual, Politics, and Power.* New Haven, CT: Yale University Press.

Klein, Daniel, E., 1997, "Promise Keeping in the Great Society," in *Reputation: Studies in the Voluntary Elicitation of Good Conduct*, Daniel E Klein (ed.). Ann Arbor: The University of Michigan Press.

Lagergren, Fredrika, 1999, *På andra sidan välfärdsstaten: En studie i politiska idéers betydelse.* Diss. Gothenburg: University of Gothenburg, Department of Political Science.

Lantz, Göran, 1977, *Eigentumsrecht–ein Recht oder ein Unrecht? Eine kritische Beurteilung der ethischen Argumente fuer das Privateigenthum bei Aristoteles, Thomas von Aquino, Grotius, Locke, Hegel, Marx und in den modernen katholischen Sozialenzykliken*. Diss. Uppsala: Almqvist & Wiksell International.

—, 1996, "Människan, hemmet och tingen," in *Hemmet i vården–vården i hemmet*, David Gaunt and Göran Lantz (eds.). Stockholm: Liber.

—, 2000. "Applied Ethics: What Kind of Ethics and What Kind of Ethicist?" in *Journal of Applied Philosophy*, vol. 17, no. 1.

Larmore, Charles, 1996, *The Morality of Modernity*. Cambridge: Cambridge University Press.

Lash, Christopher, 1978, *The Culture of Narcissism*. New York: Norton.

Lefebvre, G., 1964, *The French Revolution*. 2 vols. Transl. by J. Hall Stewart and J. Friguglietti. London: Routledge and Kegan Paul.

Leopold, David, 1995, "Introduction," in *Stirner: The Ego and its Own*. Cambridge: Cambridge University Press.

Lucas, C. (ed.), 1988, *The Political Culture of the French Revolution*. Vol. 2 of *The French Revolution and the Creation of Modern Political Culture*. Oxford: Pergamon Press.

Lundstrom, Tommy and Filip Wijkstrom, 1998, *The Nonprofit Sector in Sweden*. Manchester: University of Manchester Press.

Mably, G.B., 1789, *Oeuvres completes de l'abbé de Mably*. London.

Macedo, Stephen, 1991, *Liberal Virtues: Citizenship, Virtue and Community in Liberal Constitutionalism*. Oxford: Clarendon Press.

MacIntyre, Alasdair and Paul Ricoeur, 1969, *The Religious Significance of Atheism*. New York and London: Columbia University Press.

—, 1981, *After Virtue: A Study in Moral Theory*. Notre Dame, IN: University of Notre Dame Press.

—, 1999. *Dependent Rational Animals: Why Human Beings Need the Virtues*. London: Duckworth.

Malmberg, Torsten, 1980, *Human Territoriality: Survey of Behavioural Territories in Man with Preliminary Analysis and Discussion of Meaning*. The Hague: Mouton.

—, 1983, *Räkna med revir: om människans beteende vid uppdelningen av rummet*. Stockholm: Liber.

—, 1986, *House as a Territory: A Pilot Study into the Behavioural Territoriality of Human Buildings*. Lund.

Manson, John Hope, 1997, "Originality: Moral Good, Private Vice or Self-Enchantment?" in *Jean-Jacques Rousseau and the Sources of the Self,* John Hope Manson (ed.). Aldershot: Avebury/Ashgate.

Mason, Andrew, 1990, "Autonomy, Liberalism and State Neutrality," in *Philosophical Quarterly,* vol. 40.

Mathiez, A., 1927, *La vie chère et le mouvement social sous la Terreur*. Paris: Payot.

Melöe, Jakob, 1993a, "Remaking a Form of Life," lecture, The 10th Scandinavian Philosophy Symposium, Harjattulla, Turku, 20-22 August 1993.

—, 1993b, "Steder". Paper presented at *Kystseminariet*, September 1993.

Merleau-Ponty, Maurice, 1995, *Phenomenology of Perception.*, Transl. C. Smith. London: Routledge.

Meyers, Diana, 1989, *Self, Society and Personal Choice*. New York: Columbia University Press.

Möller, Göran, 1998, *Ethics and the Life of Faith*. Leuven: Peeters.

Montesquieu, Charles de Secondat, Baron de [1748] 1950-1961, *De l'ésprit des lois*. Critical edition by J. Brethe de la Gressaye. Paris.

Murphy, Liam, 1998, "Institutions and the demands of justice," in *Philosophy and Public Affairs*, vol. 27.

Nagel, Thomas, 1991, *Equality and Partiality.* Oxford: Oxford University Press.

Necker, J., 1792, *Du Pouvoir Exécutif dans les Grands États.* 2 vol. Paris.

Nehamas, Alexander, 1994, "Pity and Fear in the *Rhetoric* and the *Poetics*," in *Aristotle's Rhetoric*, David Furley & Alexander Nehamas (eds.). Princeton, NJ: Princeton University Press.

Nietzsche, Friedrich, 1973, *Beyond Good and Evil.* Harmondsworth: Penguin.

Nozick, Robert, 1974, *Anarchy, State, and Utopia.* Oxford: Blackwell.

Nussbaum, Martha, 1986, *The Fragility of Goodness: Luck and Ethics in Greek Tragedy and Philosophy.* Cambridge and New York: Cambridge University Press.

—, 1988, "Non-Relative Virtues: An Aristotelian Approach," in *Midwest Studies in Philosophy*, Peter A. French et al. (eds.), vol. 13.

—, 1996, "Compassion: The Basic Social Emotion," in *Social Philosophy and Policy Foundation*, vol. 13.

O'Neill, Onora, 1996, *Towards Justice and Virtue.* Cambridge: Cambridge University Press.

Okin, Susan Miller, 1999, *Is Multiculturalism Bad for Women?* Princeton, NJ: Princeton University Press.

Olivecrona, Karl, 1969, "The Concept of a Right According to Grotius and Pufendorf," in *Rechtsfindung. Beiträge zur juristischen Methodenlehre. Festschrift für Oscar Adolf Germann zum 80 Geburtstag*, Peter Noll and Günter Stratenwerth (eds.). Bern.

—, 1974, "Locke's Theory of Appropriation," in *Philosophical Quaterly*, vol. 19.

Österberg, Dag, 1977, *Makt och materiell.* Göteborg: Korpen.

Ostrom, Elinor, 1990, *Governing the Commons: The Evolution of Institutions for Collective Action.* Cambridge: Cambridge University Press.

Pearce, Jone L., 1993, *Volunteers: The Organizational Behavior of Unpaid Workers.* London and New York: Routledge.

Pincoffs, Edmund L., 1986, *Quandaries and Virtures: Against Reductivism in Ethics.* Lawrence, KS: University Press of Kansas.

Pocock, J.G.A., 1985, *Virtue, Commerce, and History: Essays on Political Thought and History, Chiefly in the Eighteenth Century.* Cambridge: Cambridge University Press.

Przeworski, Adam, 1985, *Capitalism and Social Democracy.* Cambridge: Cambridge University Press.

— and Henry Teune, 1970, *The Logic of Comparative Social Inquiry.* New York: John Wiley & Sons.

Putnam, Robert, 1993, *Making Democracy Work: Civic Traditions in Modern Italy.* Princeton, NJ: Princeton University Press.

—, 1995, "Bowling Alone: America's declining social capital," in *Journal of Democracy*, vol. 6.

Rawls, John, 1971, *A Theory of Justice.* Oxford: Oxford University Press.

—, 1993, *Political Liberalism.* New York: Columbia University Press.

Raz, Joseph, 1986, *The Morality of Freedom.* Oxford: Clarendon Press.

Redvall, Christina, 1987, *Bostadens estetik: om relationen mellan människa och bostad.* Gothenburg: Chalmers tekniska högskola, Avd. för bostadsplanering.

Ricoeur, Paul, 1991, "Life: A Story in Search of a Narrator," in *A Ricoeur Reader: Reflection and Imagination*, Mario J. Valdés (ed.). Toronto: Harverster Wheatsheaf.

Robbins, Caroline, 1959, *The Eighteenth-Century Commonwealthman.* Cambridge, MA.

Robespierre, M.M.I., 1910-67, *Oeuvres completes de Robespierre.* Ed. E. Hamel. Paris.

Rosenblum, Nancy L., 1998, *Membership and Morals.* Princeton, NJ: Princeton University Press.

Rotberg, Robert (ed.), 2001, *Patterns of Social Capital: Stability and Change in Historical Perspective.* Cambridge: Cambridge University Press.

Rousseau, Jean Jacques, 1962, *The Political Writings of Jean Jacques Rousseau.* Introduction and notes by C.E. Vaughan. 2 vols. Oxford: Blackwell.

Russell, Bertrand, 1925, "The Free Man's Worship," in *Mysticism and Logic*. London: Longman Green.

Saint-Just, A.L.L. de, 1984, *Oeuvres complètes*. Ed., M. Duval. Paris: G. Lebovici.

Salamon, Lester and Helmut Anheier, 1999, "The Third World's Third Sector in Comparative Perspective," in *International Perspectives on Voluntary Action Reshaping the Third Sector*, David Lewis (ed.). London: Earthscan.

Savile, Anthony, 1982, *The Test of Time: An Essay in Philosophical Aesthetics*. Oxford: Clarendon Press.

Scheffler, Samuel, 2001, *Boundaries and Allegiances*. Oxford: Oxford University Press.

Schick, Theodore W. Jr., 1982, "Can Fictional Literature Communicate Knowledge?" in *Journal of Aesthetic Education*, vol. 16.

Scott, Joanna and Judith Stark, 1996, *Love and Saint Augustine*. Chicago and London: University of Chicago Press.

Sharpe, Robert A., 1997, "One Sheer for Simulation Theory," in *Inquiry*, vol. 40.

Sherman, Nancy, 1989, *The Fabric of Character: Aristotle's Theory of Virtue*. Oxford: Oxford University Press.

Sieyès, E. J., 1989, *Oeuvres de Sieyès*. Paris: EDHIS.

Singer, Peter, 1972, "Famine, affluence and morality," in *Philosophy and Public Affairs*, vol. 1.

Skocpol, Theda, 1999, "How Americans became Civic," in *Civic Engagement in American Democracy*, in Theda Skocpol and Morris P. Fiorina (eds.), Washington, DC and New York: Brookings Institution Press and Russell Sage Foundation.

Slote, Michael, 1988, "Critical Notice," in *Canadian Journal of Philosophy*, vol. 18.

Smith, Adam, 1976, *The Theory of Moral Sentiments*, D. D. Raphael and A. L. Macfie (eds.). Oxford: Clarendon Press.

Smith, Tara, 1999, "Justice as a Personal Virtue," in *Social Theory and Practice*, vol. 25.

Soboul, A, 1964, *The Parisian Sans-Culottes and the French Revolution*. Transl. by G. Lewis. Oxford: Oxford University Press.

Stears, Mark, 1999, "Needs, Welfare and the Limits of Associationalism," in *Economy and Society*, vol. 28.

Stolle, Dietlind, 1998, "Bowling Together, Bowling Alone: The Development of Generalized Trust in Voluntary Associations," in *Political Psychology*, vol. 19 (September), p. 500.

Taylor, Charles, 1985, "What's Wrong with Negative Liberty," in *Philosophy and the Human Sciences, Philosophical Papers 2*. Cambridge: Cambridge University Press.

—, 1985, *Human Agency and Language: Philosophical Papers 1*. Cambridge: Cambridge University Press.

—, 1989, *The Sources of the Self*. Cambridge: Cambridge University Press.

—, 1991, *The Ethics of Authenticity*. New Haven: Yale University Press.

—, 1993, "The Motivation Behind a Procedural Ethics," in *Kant and Modern Political Philosophy*, Ronald Beiner and William James Booth (eds.). New Haven & London: Yale University Press.

—, 1995a, "The Politics of Recognition," in *Philosophical Arguments*. Cambridge, MA: Harvard University Press.

—, 1995b. "Irreducible Social Goods," in *Philosophical Arguments*. Cambridge, MA: Harvard University Press.

Thiébaut, Carlos, 1997, "The Logic of Autonomy and the Logic of Authenticity," in *Philosophy and Social Criticism*, vol. 23.

Thomas, Laurence, 1989, *Living Morally: A Psychology of Moral Character*. Philadelphia, PA: Temple University Press.

Thompson, J., 1939, *Robespierre*. Oxford: Blackwell.

Tocqueville, Alexis de, 1968, *Democracy in America*. Glasgow: Collins.

Todd, Janet, 2000, *Mary Wollstonecraft: A Revolutionary Life.* London: Weidenfeld & Nicolson.

Tolstoy, Leo, 1960, *The Death of Ivan Ilyich and Other Stories*, Transl. Rosemary Edmonds. Harmondsworth: Penguin.

Transparency International. Annual Report 2000. Berlin: Transparency International.

Tuan, Yi-Fu, 1974, *Topophilia: A Study of Environmental Perception, Attitudes, and Values.* Englewood Cliffs, NJ: Prentice-Hall.

Turner, Bryan, S., 1991, *Religion and Social Theory.* London: Sage.

—, 2001, "The Erosion of Citizenship," in *British Journal of Sociology*, vol. 52.

Uddhammar, Emil and Fredrik Erixon, 2002, *Kapitalism, nätverk och demokrati: förutsättningar för samarbete och myter om socialt kapital.* Stockholm: City University Press.

Unger, Peter, 1996, *Living High and Letting Die.* New York: Oxford University Press.

Uslander, Eric, 2000-01, "Producing and Consuming Trust," in *Political Science Quarterly*, vol. 115:4, pp. 569-90.

Van Kley, D., 1996, *The Religious Origins of the French Revolution: From Calvin to the Civil Constitution 1560-1781.* New Haven: Yale University Press.

Veblen, Thorstein, 1994, *The Theory of the Leisure Class.* London: Penguin Books.

Verene, Donald, 1997, *Philosophy and the Return to Self-Knowledge.* New Haven, CT: Yale University Press.

Wasserman, Stanley and Katherine Faust, 1994, *Social Network Analysis.* Cambridge, MA: Cambridge University Press.

Weber, Max, 1958, *The Religion of India.* New York: Free Press.

—, 1978, *Economy and Society.* Berkeley and Los Angeles, CA: University of California Press.

Weil, Simone, 1978, *The Need for Roots.* London: Routledge.

Wetzel, J., 1992, *Augustine and the Limits of Virtue.* Cambridge: Cambridge University Press.

White, Steven A., 1992, *Sovereign Virtue: Aristotle on the Relation between Happiness and Prosperity.* Stanford, CA: Stanford University Press.

Williams, Andrew, 1998, "Incentives, Inequality, and Publicity," in *Philosophy and Public Affairs*, vol. 27.

Wokler, Robert, 1997, "Deconstructing the Self on the Wild Side," in *Jean-Jacques Rousseau and the Sources of the Self*, John Hope Manson (ed.). Avebury: Aldershot.

Wollstonecraft Mary and William Godwin, 1987, *A Short Residence in Sweden, and Memoires of the Author of 'The Rights of Women'*, Richard Holmes (ed.). Harmondsworth: Penguin Books.

Woodruff, Paul, 1999, "Paideia and Good Judgment," in *Philosophy of Education*, David M. Steiner (ed.). Vol. 3 of the *Proceedings of the Twentieth World Congress of Philosophy.*

—, 2001, *Reverence: Renewing a Forgotten Virtue.* New York: Oxford University Press.

—, "Natural Justice," in *Presocratic Philosophy*, Victor Caston (ed.) (forthcoming).

World Development Indicators, 2000. Washington, DC: The World Bank.

Wuthnow, R., 1996, *Poor Richard's Principle: Recovering the American Dream through the Moral Dimension of Work, Business, and Money.* Princeton, NJ: Princeton University Press.

—, 1991, *Acts of Compassion: Caring for Others and Helping Ourselves.* Princeton, NJ: Princeton University Press.

Yamagishi, Toshio and Midori Yamagishi, 1994, "Trust and commitment in the United States and Japan," in *Motivation and Emotion*, vol. 18, no. 2, pp. 129-66.

About the Contributors

Ludvig Beckman is a Ph.D. in political science at the Department of Government, Uppsala University. He is the author of *The Liberal State and the Politics of Virtue* (Transaction Publishers, 2001).

John Dunn is a fellow of King's College, Cambridge, and professor of political theory. He has written or edited eighteen books about topics ranging from John Locke to democracy, modern revolution, and the contemporary politics of Japan, Korea, and Ghana.

Katarina Elam is a Ph.D. in aesthetics, and a lecturer and researcher at the Department of ALM, Aesthetics and Cultural Studies, Uppsala University.

Göran Lantz is consulting professor in health care ethics, Uppsala University and director of the Ersta Institute for Health Care Ethics in Stockholm.

Göran Möller is associate professor in ethics at the University of Uppsala and investigator at the Church of Sweden. His books include *Ethics and the Life of Faith: A Christian Moral Perspective* (Peeters, 1998).

Ruth Scurr holds a British Academy Postdoctoral Fellowship at the Faculty of Social and Political Sciences, University of Cambridge.

Bryan S. Turner is professor of sociology and head of department, University of Cambridge. Recent publications include *The Blackwell Companion to Social Theory* (Blackwell's, 2000) and *Society and Culture, Scarcity and Solidarity* (Sage, 2001).

Emil Uddhammar is associate professor and research director at the Ax:son Johnson Foundation in Stockholm. He is presently conducting research on identity and globalization, and is one of the editors of *Axess*.

Paul Woodruff is Thompson Professor in the Humanities at the Department of Philosophy, University of Texas. His recent publications include *Reverence: Renewing a Forgotten Virtue* (Oxford University Press, 2001) and *Antigone* (Hackett, 2001).

Index

For Product Safety Concerns and Information please contact our EU
representative GPSR@taylorandfrancis.com
Taylor & Francis Verlag GmbH, Kaufingerstraße 24, 80331 München, Germany

www.ingramcontent.com/pod-product-compliance
Lightning Source LLC
Chambersburg PA
CBHW050611280326
41932CB00016B/2992